Refusing to Behave in
Early Modern Literature

Edinburgh Critical Studies in Renaissance Culture

Series Editors: Lorna Hutson, Katherine Ibbett, Joe Moshenska and Kathryn Murphy

Titles available in the series:

Open Subjects: English Renaissance Republicans, Modern Selfhoods and the Virtue of Vulnerability
James Kuzner

The Phantom of Chance: From Fortune to Randomness in Seventeenth-Century French Literature
John D. Lyons

Don Quixote in the Archives: Madness and Literature in Early Modern Spain
Dale Shuger

Untutored Lines: The Making of the English Epyllion
William P. Weaver

The Girlhood of Shakespeare's Sisters: Gender, Transgression, Adolescence
Jennifer Higginbotham

Friendship's Shadows: Women's Friendship and the Politics of Betrayal in England, 1640–1705
Penelope Anderson

Inventions of the Skin: The Painted Body in Early English Drama, 1400–1642
Andrea Ria Stevens

Performing Economic Thought: English Drama and Mercantile Writing, 1600–1642
Bradley D. Ryner

Forgetting Differences: Tragedy, Historiography and the French Wars of Religion
Andrea Frisch

Listening for Theatrical Form in Early Modern England
Allison Deutermann

Theatrical Milton: Politics and Poetics of the Staged Body
Brendan Prawdzik

Legal Reform in English Renaissance Literature
Virginia Lee Strain

The Origins of English Revenge Tragedy
George Oppitz-Trotman

Crime and Consequence in Early Modern Literature and Law
Judith Hudson

Shakespeare's Golden Ages: Resisting Nostalgia in Elizabethan Drama
Kristine Johanson

Refusing to Behave in Early Modern Literature
Laura Seymour

Visit the Edinburgh Critical Studies in Renaissance Culture website at www.edinburghuniversitypress.com/series/ECSRC

Refusing to Behave in Early Modern Literature

Laura Seymour

EDINBURGH
University Press

Edinburgh University Press is one of the leading university presses in the UK. We publish academic books and journals in our selected subject areas across the humanities and social sciences, combining cutting-edge scholarship with high editorial and production values to produce academic works of lasting importance. For more information visit our website: edinburghuniversitypress.com

© Laura Seymour 2023, 2024

Edinburgh University Press Ltd
The Tun – Holyrood Road
12(2f) Jackson's Entry
Edinburgh EH8 8PJ

First published in hardback by Edinburgh University Press 2023

Typeset in 10.5/13 Adobe Sabon by
Cheshire Typesetting Ltd, Cuddington, Cheshire

A CIP record for this book is available from the British Library

ISBN 978 1 4744 9180 8 (hardback)
ISBN 978 1 4744 9181 5 (paperback)
ISBN 978 1 4744 9182 2 (webready PDF)
ISBN 978 1 4744 9183 9 (epub)

The right of Laura Seymour to be identified as the author of this work has been asserted in accordance with the Copyright, Designs and Patents Act 1988, and the Copyright and Related Rights Regulations 2003 (SI No. 2498).

Contents

Acknowledgements	vi
Series Editor's Preface	viii
Introduction: The Body at Play in Early Modern Texts	1
1. Ungracious Grace: Proprioception and Staging Taste in Thomas Dekker's *If This Be Not a Good Play, the Devil Is in It* (1611)	8
2. Walking Without God – (Mis)Learning Through the Gait in Mateo Alemán's *Guzmán de Alfarache* (1599 and 1604) and James Mabbe's *The Rogue* (1622)	36
3. Plain Plasticity – Thomas Ellwood's *The History of the Life of Thomas Ellwood* (1714)	58
4. Chaste and Silent – Again. Vitality and the Bound and Loosed Body in I.T.'s *Grim the Collier of Croydon; or, The Devil and His Dame* (c. 1600)	81
Index	109

Acknowledgements

I was very fortunate to pass many of the 7 years I spent researching and writing this book alongside academic and administrative colleagues at Birkbeck, University of London and St Anne's College, Oxford; thank you to you all. My warm thanks most of all go to Gillian Woods who has always been a source of support and wise guidance; thank you Gill for the opportunities you have given me to present my research over the years. Thank you very much to Susan Wiseman, Isabel Davis, Peter Fifield, Laura Salisbury, Eva Lauenstein, Judith Hudson and Heike Bauer for their encouragement, example of brilliant scholarship, and advice as I pursued my research. Thank you to Raphael Lyne, Amy Cook, Tim Chesters, Kathryn Banks, Rhonda Blair, Guillemette Bolens, and Ellen Spolsky, and to all members of the Cognitive Futures in the Humanities network for their wonderfully inspiring research and conversation and the opportunities they provided me to develop the ideas in this book. Thank you to Mercedes Rodríguez-Rubio Camacho, to Harper Dafforn who proofread the finished typescript and to Victoria García Marín who kindly proofread an early version of Chapter 2. Thank you to all of the students who have discussed the themes and texts in this book with me in various classes and to Clare Thomas and all others who administratively supported my research.

Many thanks to all the editors at EUP; thank you Lorna Hutson, Joe Moshenska, Michelle Houston, and Susannah Butler. Lorna put a huge amount of effort into helping me improve this book, for which I am very grateful. Thank you to the librarians and archivists at Oxford, Birkbeck, the Biblioteca Nacional, and the Friends Library in London.

I could not have completed this book without the financial support of my family members, a medical humanities small grant from the Wellcome Trust which enabled me to research Chapter 3, and research support money from Birkbeck which enabled me to travel to Spain to research Chapter 2. Nor could I have completed it without the NHS, specifically the care of the oncology department at Cheltenham General Hospital, and of the Bristol Autism Spectrum Service which helped me to become (albeit precariously and intermittently) one of the 22% or thereabouts of autistic people in the UK with a job. Finally, and far from least, I could not have completed this book without my friends and loved ones, thank you to you all. Thank you to Meredith Knowles and Xin Xu, and to Stuart Bell for your friendship and German help. Love and thank you to Sandy Steel, and most of all to my wife Martha Sofía Franco Rodríguez – to her I dedicate my book.

Series Editor's Preface

Edinburgh Critical Studies in Renaissance Culture may, as a series title, provoke some surprise. On the one hand, the choice of the word 'culture' (rather than, say, 'literature') suggests that writers in this series subscribe to the now widespread assumption that the 'literary' is not isolable, as a mode of signifying, from other signifying practices that make up what we call 'culture'. On the other hand, most of the critical work in English literary studies of the period 1500–1700 which endorses this idea has rejected the older identification of the period as 'the Renaissance', with its implicit homage to the myth of essential and universal Man coming to stand (in all his sovereign individuality) at the centre of a new world picture. In other words, the term 'culture' in the place of 'literature' leads us to expect the words 'early modern' in the place of 'Renaissance'. Why, then, 'Edinburgh Critical Studies in *Renaissance Culture*'?

The answer to that question lies at the heart of what distinguishes this critical series and defines its parameters. As Terence Cave has argued, the term 'early modern', though admirably egalitarian in conception, has had the unfortunate effect of essentialising the modern, that is, of positing 'the advent of a once-and-for-all modernity' which is the deictic 'here and now' from which we look back.[1] The phrase 'early modern', that is to say, forecloses the possibility of other modernities, other futures that might have arisen, narrowing the scope of what we may learn from the past by construing it as a narrative leading inevitably to Western modernity, to 'us'. *Edinburgh Critical Studies in Renaissance Culture* aims rather to shift the emphasis from a story of progress – early modern to modern – to a series of critical encounters and conversations with the past, which may reveal to us some surprising alternatives buried within texts familiarly construed as episodes on the way to certain identifying features of our endlessly fascinating modernity. In keeping

[1] Terence Cave, 'Locating the Early Modern', *Paragraph*, 29:1 (2006) 12–26, 14.

with one aspect of the etymology of 'Renaissance' or 'Rinascimento' as 'rebirth', moreover, this series features books that explore and interpret anew elements of the critical encounter between writers of the period 1500–1700 and texts of Greco-Roman literature, rhetoric, politics, law, oeconomics, *eros* and friendship.

The term 'culture', then, indicates a license to study and scrutinise objects other than literary ones, and to be more inclusive about both the forms and the material and political stakes of making meaning both in the past and in the present. 'Culture' permits a realisation of the benefits to be reaped after two decades of interdisciplinary enrichment in the arts. No longer are historians naïve about textual criticism, about rhetoric, literary theory or about readerships; likewise, literary critics trained in close reading now also turn easily to court archives, to legal texts, and to the historians' debates about the languages of political and religious thought. Social historians look at printed pamphlets with an eye for narrative structure; literary critics look at court records with awareness of the problems of authority, mediation and institutional procedure. Within these developments, modes of research that became unfashionable and discredited in the 1980s – for example, studies in classical or vernacular 'source texts', or studies of literary 'influence' across linguistic, confessional and geographical boundaries – have acquired a new critical edge and relevance as the convergence of the disciplines enables the unfolding of new cultural histories (that is to say, what was once studied merely as 'literary influence' may now be studied as a fraught cultural encounter). The term 'Renaissance' thus retains the relevance of the idea of consciousness and critique within these textual engagements of past and present, and, while it foregrounds the Western European experience, is intended to provoke comparativist study of wider global perspectives rather than to promote the 'universality' of a local, if far-reaching, historical phenomenon. Finally, as traditional pedagogic boundaries between 'Medieval' and 'Renaissance' are being called into question by cross disciplinary work emphasising the 'reformation' of social and cultural forms, so this series, while foregrounding the encounter with the classical past, is self-conscious about the ways in which that past is assimilated to the projects of Reformation and Counter-Reformation, spiritual, political and domestic, that finally transformed Christendom into Europe.

Individual books in this series vary in methodology and approach, sometimes blending the sensitivity of close literary analysis with incisive, informed and urgent theoretical argument, at other times offering critiques of grand narratives of the period by their work in manuscript transmission, or in the archives of legal, social and architectural history, or by social histories of gender and childhood. What all these books have in common, however, is the capacity to offer compelling, well-documented and lucidly written critical accounts of how writers and thinkers in the period 1500–1700 reshaped, transformed and critiqued the texts and practices of their world, prompting new perspectives on what we think we have learned from them.

Lorna Hutson, Katherine Ibbett,
Joe Moshenska and Kathryn Murphy

Introduction: The Body at Play in Early Modern Texts

In his autobiographical *The History of the Life of Thomas Ellwood*, the Quaker Thomas Ellwood describes a decisive encounter with his aggressively anti-Quaker father, Walter Ellwood.[1] Reflecting on his life from a delicate youth to an adult Quaker, Thomas's *History* was published in 1714, about a year after he passed away, his funeral attended by 'a large company' of Quakers.[2] In the decisive moment I wish to draw our attention to, Thomas runs from the family home, bent on attending a Quaker meeting, and unable to take any more of Walter's intolerance towards his faith. Walter pursues Thomas, determined to stop him engaging in Quaker worship. Describing his and Walter's parting, Thomas does not record them exchanging words; rather he dwells on their bodies as they move on Walter's ground: chasing and copying each other, spurring each other on. As the son disobeys his father, he revels in representing the superior power of his youthful body; readers might laugh at Thomas's slightly patronising recollection that Walter, venerable Justice of the Peace and patriarch, 'held to it for a while':

> observing that my Father gained Ground upon me, I somewhat mended my Pace. This he observing, mended his Pace also; and at length Ran. Whereupon I ran also; and a fair Course we had, through a large Meadow of his, which lay behind his House and of sight of the Town. He was not, I suppose, then above Fifty Years of Age; and being light of Body, and nimble of Foot, he held to it for a while. But afterwards slacking his Pace to take Breath, and observing that I had gotten Ground of him; he turned back, and went home.[3]

'A fair Course we had.' If we did not know the context, we might read this encounter as a friendly race, dance, show of kinship through bodies mirroring each other, act of intra-familial mockery, or two people expending energy for the fun and exhilaration of it. It is striking that Thomas slows his narrative to focus narrowly on the complex (inter)play of he and Walter's bodies in the midst of sectarian and familial strife.

Thomas uses textual features – specifically polyptoton and the stop and start of meaningfully linked clauses – to represent the rhythm of his and Walter's bodily interactions. Though each man's activity is initially contained within his own clause, language shared between clauses ('mended my/his Pace', 'ran') shows Thomas and Walter's discrete bodies influencing each other. Traditionally the father teaches the son, but here – as if in a final attempt to influence each other's behaviours after months of arguing – they take it in turns to take their cues from each other: as Thomas 'mended [his] pace', Walter copies him and 'mended his pace'; as Walter 'Ran', Thomas responds and 'ran also'. This accelerated movement carries across full stops as Thomas and Walter's observations of each other incite them to increase their speed. In sync for a moment, father and son come to share a clause, 'a fair Course we had'. The text reveals the ways in which Thomas's body energetically serves him well and enables him to escape whilst Walter's body, permeable to Thomas's influence, lets Walter down. Though the disciplinarian Walter had set himself up as arbiter of proper (i.e., non-Quaker) behaviour at home, Walter's body refuses to behave as he wishes. As we shall see later in this book, Thomas writes his *History* in a specific Quaker prose style: 'plain and true', and devoted to presenting Quakers positively and in particular as steadfast in the face of suffering. Thomas's last image of his father is telling: exhausted physically and perhaps emotionally, Walter fades into the distance as Thomas continues on his Quaker quest, the hero of his own story.

This book examines the interrelation of the bodily and the textual in four early modern literary examples of bad behaviour. In these examples, as with Thomas and Walter's encounter above, the text maps and is shaped by the idiosyncrasies of individual bodies as they collide with the values of small communities like the sect, social milieu, religious brotherhood, or family. Two of the literary examples I focus on in this book, Thomas Dekker's *If This Be Not a Good Play, the Devil Is in It* (1611) and the anonymous *Grim the Collier of Croydon* (c. 1600, attributed to 'I. T.'), are dramatic texts. These plays implicate actors' bodies in textual representations of corporeal behaviours like eating, saying grace, swooning, raging, and demonic possession. The other two examples are prose works whose textual rhythms enable us to see the body in all its influenced and influential glory: Ellwood's *History* and Mateo Alemán's picaresque novel *Guzmán de Alfarache* (1599–1604), translated into English by James Mabbe as *The Rogue* (1622). I examine the ways in which Dekker, Ellwood, Alemán, Mabbe, and Anon all use textual tricks to provoke bodily responses in readers, drawing on readers' bodily experiences to enrich their textual descriptions.

These literary texts are fruitful to study because by comically exaggerating and slowing down to describe bodily behaviours, they enable us to see them in a new, insightful light. By making everyday, automatic bodily behaviours strange, these texts call on us to reflect on, and better understand, how habitual actions shaped and revealed the thoughts and intentions of early modern individuals. The philosopher and cognitive theorist Maxine Sheets-Johnstone argues in *The Primacy of Movement* (1998) that we barely think about most of our habitual behaviours, and thus only come to notice and reflect on the normal through conscious change:

> we need only try different ways of doing something habitual—something like walking, for example, changing not only our leg swings, for instance, by initiating movement from our ankle joints by a spring action rather than from our hip joints, but changing our arm swing, the curvature of our spine, the cadence of our walk, the amplitude of our step and so on [. . .] Just such oddness jars us into an awareness of what we qualitatively marginalize in our habitual ways of doing things. By making the familiar strange, we familiarize ourselves anew with the familiar.[4]

By examining bad behaviour (which makes for a good story) and 'making the familiar strange', the literary texts I examine in this book draw norms into sharp relief. The behaviours I examine in this book – saying grace, walking around town, hat-doffing, sitting quietly – were generally unremarkable aspects of everyday life, no doubt often performed by rote, or without much thought. Indeed it was this very possibility of unthinking repetition that could make them such powerful tools of social control.

Terence Cave writes in *Thinking with Literature* (2016) that literary texts 'alter [our] cognitive environment' by affecting our capacity for inference.[5] Cave argues that literature enables us properly to notice life; usually, life is on the move and we only notice it fleetingly because we too are alive and on the move. Walking is one of Sheets-Johnstone's favourite examples of a movement that we rarely notice; in Chapter 2, I turn explicitly to the ways in which literary texts enable us properly to notice walking. Sheets-Johnstone describes the 'kinaesthetic melodies' of habitual actions like (to follow her examples) walking and brushing our teeth: these are the tempos and arrangements of movements needed to perform these actions. Literary texts have their own melody, created through the arrangement of words and clauses and poetic effects like enjambment; applying literary-critical skills to texts describing bodily behaviours enables us to scrutinise these behaviours insofar as they appear in, and shape and are shaped by, the text.

Cognitive literary theorists like Cave and Guillemette Bolens examine the ways in which texts engage readers and audiences' bodily responses, suggesting a fruitful interplay between the bodily and textual. Cave describes understanding others' intentions in terms of 'reading' their bodies,

> When you try to guess someone's intentions, or their mental habit, or their social attitude, from their posture and gesture, motor resonance will always be there, a slight but distinct sensation that allows you to feel something like what it is to be that person, where they're coming from; their very language may have 'fingers', too, touching you in unexpected places. You put all that together with other information, maybe prolonging the analysis by means of conscious reflection, either silently, on your own, or in dialogue with others. However you do it, you're not in fact reading abstractly remote 'minds': what you read is bodies, together with all of the elusive, often hidden, thinking that human bodies do.[6]

Naomi Rokotnitz puts this in terms of trusting, and empathising through, the body; relying on the body to tell us im-mediately what a text or moment means.[7]

In her key study *The Style of Gestures* (2012, translated from her 2008 *Le Style des gestes*), Bolens explains how we can understand literary texts through two linked types of bodily knowledge: kinesic intelligence and kinaesthetic knowledge. Kinesic intelligence is 'our human capacity to discern and interpret body movements, body postures, gestures, and facial expressions'; kinaesthetic knowledge is knowledge we draw from sensing our own body spatially, and in motion.[8] Bolens affirms that kinesic and kinaesthetic knowledges support each other, enabling us to communicate with other people: we interpret the movements we observe other bodies making because our kinaesthetic knowledge of our own movements empowers us to 'infer' that others feel as we do when moving in a certain way, 'I cannot feel the kinaesthetic sensations in another person's arm', she writes, 'yet I may infer his kinaesthetic sensations on the basis of the kinesic signals I perceive in his movements. In an act of kinaesthetic empathy, I may internally simulate what these inferred sensations possibly feel like via my own kinaesthetic memory and knowledge.'[9] In *L'humour et le savoir des corps* (2016), echoing Sheets-Johnstone's musical notion of the body's 'kinaesthetic melody', Bolens adduces muscle 'tone' (both tension and musicality) as something that enables us to infer others' thoughts, intentions, and feelings.[10] The literary texts I examine describe characters using kinesic and kinaesthetic learning and imagining to apprehend the world and other people. These texts also prompt, and avail themselves of, readers' kinaesthetic understandings; Bolens draws on scientific studies of how reading action-words related to the body (like 'kick') can provoke corresponding sensorimotor responses in the reader.[11] Inspired by Bolens's work, I argue that when confronted with a description of a literary character behaving in a particular way, we 'read' their behaviour using a mix of literary critical skills and our own bodily experience.

Chapter 1 of this book focuses on proprioception: Dekker's *If This Be Not a Good Play, the Devil Is in It* represents the kinaesthetic experiences of eating and drinking, giving them moral valence. As Dekker's oesophageal descriptions descend into throats choked and cut, his dramatic prose style relies on readers and audiences' kinaesthetic imaginations to add meaning to these descriptions. Dekker prompts us to turn to our own experiences of hunger, licking our lips, and feeling something caught annoyingly in our throat, to appreciate the monks' tormenting greed. Chapter 2 analyses the gait in the picaresque novel *Guzmán de Alfarache* by Mateo Alemán and its Jacobean English translation by James Mabbe. I trace how the body of Guzmán, Alemán's hero, dents the English and Spanish texts, his odd gait warping the prose style and his showy legs dangling over the edges of sentences. Guzmán learns through mimicry in ways that incorporate resistance to moral development; this anti-learning in *Guzmán* helps to challenge ideas of social kinesic and kinaesthetic learning. I argue that Guzmán's recalcitrantly roguish body thereby leaves more of an impression on us than any moralising sentence in the text.

As Bolens writes, kinesis is 'interactual'; Chapter 3 examines Thomas Ellwood's self-shaping through 'sensorimotor interaction' (much of it highly unpleasant), in *The History of the Life of Thomas Ellwood*.[12] Ellwood reinforces his non-conformist faith against mainstream Anglican society by testing his Quaker identity in confrontation with his father. The chapter analyses Thomas's bodily self-shaping as textual self-shaping, following established Quaker patterns of behaviour and deploying the 'plain and true' Quaker prose style to represent his confrontations with his father in terms of accepted Quaker patterns. Ellwood is concerned with presenting a coherent, clearly pro-Quaker story with body and text in sync. Chapter 4, focusing on the c. 1600 play *Grim the Collier of Croydon*, of uncertain authorship, returns to the theme of Chapter 2, namely the ways in which a moralising text and a character's recalcitrant body can tell different stories. *Grim the Collier* tells the story of a silent 'chaste' woman whose tongue is 'loosened' by the devil and then, to the applause of the men around her, 'tied' again by God working through St Dunstan. In this final chapter, I explore how audiences and readers' kinaesthetic response to a nexus of word and text – performances and metaphors of being bound and released – work to complicate any simplistic idea that constrained, silent chastity is the more desirable state. Release and loosening offer the reader and audience member a rush of energy and enthusiasm, no matter how devilish the text's moral tells us it is.

This book deals with everyday rituals and activities and, often at the same time, with supernatural events: *Grim the Collier* and *If This Be Not a Good Play* rest on the same folkloric bedrock of the devil disguised as a human causing havoc in society, twisting everyday life. All these texts make the familiar strange; the authors communicate this to us using literary skills integrated with kinesic and kinaesthetic understanding. The key power of these texts for me is that they help us to pause and see how habitual everyday life shapes us in ways that both constrain us and offer us the potential for growth, how it relates to wider social structures, makes us legible to others, and embeds us in longer narratives. When 'the familiar' is 'made strange' in the ways that these texts put into practice, it can be more easily scrutinised. Literary writing that exaggerates, slows down, and picks apart bodily behaviour makes it is easier for us to see how a gait, a doffed hat, a prayer before lunch, can shape both literary characters and present-day human beings going about their everyday lives.

Notes

1. To avoid confusion, I will call father and son by their first names; indeed many of Thomas's tribulations centred around the fact that he and Walter shared a surname.
2. 'Our friend Thomas Elwood Departed this Life at Hunger Hill & on the 4th of the same was Buried at Jordans several Publick Friends their a large company of friend & others their' [sic], Rebecca Butterfield, *Rebecca Stevens her Book. given her by Prince Butterfeild* [sic] *therein to look* (MS, dated 1744), Friends Library and Archive, London, 4r. Butterfield (also known as Rebecca Stevens), used this journal to record the births, marriages and deaths of her fellow Quakers as well as brief accounts of their meetings.
3. Thomas Ellwood, *The History of the Life of Thomas Ellwood* (London: J. Sowle, 1714), G6r.
4. Maxine Sheets-Johnstone, *The Primacy of Movement* (Amsterdam: John Benjamins, 1998), 142–3.
5. Terence Cave, *Thinking with Literature: Towards a Cognitive Criticism* (Oxford: Oxford University Press, 2016), 5.
6. Cave, *Thinking with Literature*, 30. On how 'the body is *the* text that we read throughout our evolution as a social species', see Lisa Zunshine, 'Lying Bodies of the Enlightenment', in Lisa Zunshine, ed., *Introduction to Cognitive Cultural Studies* (Baltimore: Johns Hopkins University Press, 2010) (pp. 115–33), 120. For an excellent introduction to cognitive humanities, see Amy Cook and Rhonda Blair, 'Introduction', in Amy Cook

7. and Rhonda Blair, eds, *Theatre, Performance and Cognition: Languages, Bodies, Ecologies* (Bloomsbury: Methuen, 2015), 1–15.
7. '[A] deep emotional learning that can bypass resistance, bias, and fear, often opening new avenues for communication and encouraging trust', Naomi Rokotnitz, *Trusting Performance: A Cognitive Approach to Embodiment in Drama* (New York: Palgrave, 2011), 3.
8. Guillemette Bolens, *The Style of Gestures: Embodiment and Cognition in Literary Narrative*, trans. Guillemette Bolens (Baltimore: Johns Hopkins, 2012 originally published in French [2008]), 1.
9. Bolens, *The Style of Gestures*, 2–3.
10. In writing of '[l]es variations toniques de contraction et décontraction musculaires' and muscles' 'tonicité', Bolens suggests their tension, tempo, and melody. Guillemette Bolens, *L'humour et le savoir des corps: Don Quichotte, Tristram Shandy et le rire du lecteur* (Rennes: Presses Universitaires de Rennes, 2016), 11. The term 'kinetic melody', which Bolens and other cognitive theorists also use, derives from the neurologist Alexandr Luria.
11. Bolens, *The Style of Gestures*, 12–13.
12. Bolens, *The Style of Gestures*, 2; 'Une sensorimotricité *en interaction*', Bolens, *L' humour et le savoir des corps*, 19.

Chapter 1

Ungracious Grace – Proprioception and Staging Taste in Thomas Dekker's *If This Be Not a Good Play, the Devil Is in It* (1611)

The power of the kinaesthetic imagination, defined in the introductory chapter, is demonstrated in Thomas Dekker's 1611 play, *If This Be Not a Good Play, the Devil Is in It* when a novice monk, Friar Rush, comes forward to say grace before the daytime meal in his monastery. The play is set in Naples; the group of Italian monks preparing to dine immediately suggests (to English Protestants) a long history of Protestant depictions of monks devoted to the pleasures of the flesh, especially eating and drinking, to the exclusion of all else. Dekker's company performed *If This Be Not Good* on the amphitheatre stage of London's Red Bull Theatre (located off busy St John Street). Rush may have been accompanied by an ominous firework or two – the Red Bull was famed for its noisiness and pyrotechnic special effects – and, as we shall see below, it is possible that Rush wore a prosthetic cow's tail and horns.[1] Rush is asked, as a novice, to 'say grace demurely' and 'waite on the Priors Trencher soberly', expectations he swiftly thwarts.[2] Rather than delivering a pious grace focusing the other monks' minds on God, Rush offers a grace designed to generate greedy effects in their bodies, minds, and souls. His grace prompts the monks to imagine delicious tastes and envisage their bodies stretching as they fill with abundant food. By means of this exercise in embodied imagination, the grace sends the monks' souls veering towards the fires of hell. Such a shift into eschatology – Dekker takes us from a daily pre-meal prayer to a drawn-out depiction of sinners forcibly gorged with searing, painful foods and drinks in hell – is striking and should give us pause. This chapter traces how proprioceptive language of fullness, greasiness, and heat, stemming from and fanning out from the grace, brings about this disastrous result.[3]

By staging his characters lingering over the meal preparations, Dekker draws attention to the monks' table and its loadings.[4] The cook Scumbroath announces the scene by entering ringing a bell, accompanied by Rush bringing in 'a cloth to lay'; Rush and Friar Alphege chat while setting the table.⁵ The following stage direction suggests that the monks enter and their food is placed in front of them: 'Enter Prior, Subprior, Alphege, Hillary, Rush, and other Friers. All sit: dishes brought in before'.⁶ The monks are sitting down to 'religious fare' – a sharp contrast to the meal Rush describes in his grace, which runs:

> For our bread, wine, ale and beere,
> For the piping hot meates heere:
> For brothes of sundrie tasts and sort,
> For beefe, veale, mutton, lamb, and porke.
> Greene-sawce with calfes head and bacon,
> Pig and goose, and cramd-vp capon.
> For past raiz'd stiffe with curious art,
> Pye, custard, florentine and tart.
> Bak'd rumpes, fried kidneys, and lam-stones,
> Fat sweete-breads, luscious maribones,
> Artichoke, and oyster-pyes,
> Butterd Crab, prawnes, lobsters thighes,
> Thankes be giuen for flesh and fishes,
> With this choice of tempting dishes:
> To which proface: with blythe lookes sit yee,
> Bids this Couent, much good do't yee.⁷

Short for 'bon prou vous fasse' (Middle French: 'may it do you good'), 'proface' was a word said to welcome guests, and/or to wish them well before a meal. Coming as it does at the end of a sonorously tempting 'grace', Rush's 'proface' marks an invitation to give way to greed; indeed the menu-like structure of the grace suggests that the next logical step would be to tuck in.

Rush is relying on the monks' proprioceptive imagination: their ability to imagine the feel of this food going down their gullets, the textures and tastes in their mouths. Dekker's readers and audiences might also respond bodily to the grace, based on a variety of individuating factors including our hunger levels, prior experiences, moral attitudes to food (vegans are less likely to salivate at a 'calfes head and bacon', not to mention 'beef, veale, mutton, lamb, and porke' and all the other meats) and our (in)familiarity with these early modern foodstuffs. Rush offers, for those who wish to take it up (and many of the monks do), a link between gourmandising and lasciviousness with vocabulary of 'paste raiz'd stiff', 'stones' (testes), 'thighs', and 'rumpes' (which could easily suggest sexualised human rather than animal bodies), and the sexual and religious ambiguity of 'flesh and fish'.⁸ Dekker engages what Ellen Spolsky and Bolens describe as our kinesic ability to infer how the monks are feeling; for instance we might see these characters' mouths gape and infer that they are hungry and surprised; as Spolsky puts it, 'we learn a lot by looking at others and by drawing analogies between their bodies and our own'.[9] Dekker represents taste in strongly bodily terms, emphasising that rooting taste in the body can make it a gateway to perdition; his invisible meal exemplifies what Lucy Munro calls 'taste's simultaneously bodily and immaterial dramatic status'.[10]

Dekker primes us to view the meal within a proprioceptive frame that emphasises the monks' mouths and fingers. Rush's conversation with Alphege as they lay the table centres around the monks' engagement with their own bodies: picking and sucking their teeth, licking and wiping their fingers. This highlights the monks' awareness of the information they can gain through touching their own bodies' surfaces. This in turn activates the audience's own proprioceptive sensibilities as we imagine toothpicks pivoting between teeth and bracing against fingers, mouths closing around fingers and teeth, hands manipulating cutlery:

> Alph: So: the Lord Priors napkin here, there the Subpriors: his knife and case of pick-toothes thus: as for the conuent [i.e., the rest of the monastery], let them licke their fingers in stead of wiping, and suck their teeth in steede of picking.[11]

By the time the other monks enter, Alphege's words have already trained us to see their mouths and hands as sites of eating – specifically, coated in grease, food particles, and/or saliva – rather than prayer. Though Alphege notionally presents licking and wiping, and sucking and picking, as alternatives, our kinesic imaginations are activated by all verbs, leading us to imagine all of these at once: a flurry of self-touching activity that we can feel in, and understand through, our own bodies.

These are not bodies eating in the wild; this is a literary, dramatic text. Indeed, the fact that the grace is double-prefixed (the name 'Rush' appears at the start and end of the grace though nobody else speaks in between), suggests a theatrical flourish. Double-prefixing often indicated that the actor was reading from a document used as a prop; Rush likely presents or unrolls a physical menu from hell.[12] Rush uses literary devices to point at, and activate, proprioceptive responses in the hungry monks; the same literary devices may activate responses in readers and audiences. Most of the play does not rhyme, making Rush's use of rhyming couplets for his grace striking – and purposeful. Rush's rhymes invite the monks to keep craning expectantly towards the next image: what new delicacy will appear in the couplet's second line to rhyme with the food in the first? We might presume that their resultantly racing imaginations get their bodies readying themselves for food – stomachs rumbling, mouths filling with saliva. Further guiding their embodied imaginative response, Rush's asyndeton suggests food piled high and/or gobbled in quick succession. His sentence structure often further evokes curious discovery; 'Greene-sawce with calfes head and bacon', for example, might suggest an order to the eating. First we notice the slathering green sauce and then once we have delved into it with knife, tongue, or hand, we discover the meat concealed beneath. Whether this line suggests viscosity and abundance (a sauce luxuriously thick enough to completely hide a calf's head), or positioning (a jug of green sauce laid beside, 'with', the accompanying meat) it is certainly an affordance, demanding visual, gustatory, interoceptive engagements on the listener's part. As 'calf's head' at this time frequently meant 'a fool', the monks here discover, or urgently desire, an image of their own foolish selves.[13]

Rush's grace is arguably extra effective at provoking greed precisely because it does not involve lavish detail. His list of foodstuffs is seasoned with just a few adjectives, such as meats in 'past raiz'd stiffe with curious art' and descriptions of the meal as 'piping hot' and the marrow-bones as 'luscious'. Rush perhaps deploys this general lack of detail, with a couple of tantalising pointers about beautiful pastry and appealing temperature, in order to prompt the monks to fill in the details with their own imaginations. As they follow his nudges and consider for themselves how the pastries, tarts, and meats will taste, their minds and desires are implicated more fully in the sin of greed. The words 'curious' and 'piping hot' (which in the seventeenth century could mean 'new') further help to keep the listeners' minds engaged: Rush does not promise the monks any old food but curiosities, novel delights.[14]

The overall effect of this grace, as I will explore throughout this chapter, is that it focuses the monks on the taste, temperature, and texture of food, rather than on thanking God for their meal. Early modern writers were very alert to the ways in which a meal could go either of two ways: grace might elevate it into a grateful spiritual experience, or diners might brutishly focus solely on filling their stomachs. Indeed some authors described greedy people who forgot the spiritual side of eating degenerating into animals; the poet Timothy Kendall states in a 1577 epigram 'Of saying grace' that one who 'sitting downe doth take his meales,| And thankes not God in grateful wise:| Goes as a brutishe Oxe to boord,| And rudely like an Asse doth rise'.[15] Kendall's point, echoed by several early modern writers is that the absence of grace makes an act of eating 'brutishe': if the eaters had only 'thanke[d] God in grateful wise', they would have been safe from waking up subhuman. Strikingly, in *If This Be Not a Good Play*, grace *is* said; the fact that it is *mis*said rather than absent causes the disaster. Dekker's play is particularly revealing because Dekker both provokes and stages bodily responses to, and traces the bodily effects of, this mis-said grace.

The Devil Saying Grace: Folklore and Oxymoron

As you may have guessed, Rush is not really a pious novice. He is, in fact, a devil, real name Shacklesoul, who has been sent into the monastery in monk disguise, to tempt the monks to sin. Shacklesoul/Rush largely succeeds in this aim: after he has captured their attention with his grace, almost all the monks give way to greed, lust, and murderous rage. The monks appoint Rush their 'maister cook' so they can feast as he has described, then they progress to drunkenness, which leads to brawls, accidental deaths, and potentially sleeping with women in the monastery. The one exception is the Subprior; immune to Rush, the Subprior accurately identifies Rush as a 'devil' and continues to follow his monastic vows. Dekker draws on an established tradition of stories about the devilish Friar Rush, shaping much of his play (and re-shaping these earlier narratives) around it. Shacklesoul/Rush is just one of the devils swarming through the play. The play opens in hell, where Pluto sends three devils called Shacklesoul, Lurchall, and Ruffman, with a further devil Glitterback on call to help them, out into the world. The devils infiltrate a monastery, merchant's office, and court respectively, to try and bring as many souls as they can back to hell. The play traces each devil's fortunes, and ends in hell, where they torment the souls they have ensnared, fittingly given the play's interest in food and drink, with painful drinks: snake venom, molten gold, and hot blood from the sinner's own heart.

Thus, though Rush's first entrance in monk-form is in the grace scene described above, Dekker has already established that he is really a devil and presented him to the audience in his demonic form as Shacklesoul, Pluto's fawning minion, protesting that he is as eager to snare human souls as a shark is to 'eate up the Fish at Sea'.[16] Considered in terms of early modern culture where grace aimed to ward off devils, it is particularly striking – even oxymoronic – to see a devil saying grace. Dekker uses strong sensory impressions firmly to fix this image, both comic in its incongruity and theologically shocking, of a devil saying grace, in the audience's minds. Shacklesoul initially 'comes up' from the hellspace through the stage trapdoor (a means of entry instantly marking him as a devil) amid loud noises including Pluto's ranting and the crack, flash, and sharp scent of the fireworks that traditionally accompanied stage devils and were a noteworthy stage-effect at the Red Bull in particular.[17]

This makes a stark contrast to the monk guise Shacklesoul/Rush later reappears in, though it is likely that during his spell in the monastery makeup and prosthetics were used to emphasise his devilishness and visually alert the audience to the oxymoron of a devil performing the Christian duty of saying grace; Shacklesoul foreshadows this when he describes himself as 'a wolfe in lambe skin leap[ing] into the rout'.[18] Taking control of the ritual of saying grace enables Shacklesoul/Rush to capture his listeners' attentions, and Dekker to make the most of the kinaesthetic and proprioceptive potential of gustatory vocabulary.

The varied speech prefixes used for this character while in his monk disguise – sometimes he is 'Rush' and sometimes 'Shack' – may have been suggestions for performance, indicating that the actor occasionally allowed the character's devilish side to show in performance and at others behaved more like a monk.[19] Rush's motivation in the grace scene is transparent: Dekker primes his audiences to see Rush unambiguously as a devil twisting a spiritual ritual; his hold on the monks' imaginations is readable as devilish possession. He also primes us to see the monks as ripe for Rush's machinations, presenting them from the outset primarily as bodies engaged in the sensory aspects of eating. Dekker thereby affords readers and audiences a privileged ability to see what the monks cannot: that the monks' self-seeing is increasingly warped by greed. The fact that the play was performed at the Red Bull, which was old monastic ground, home to several monastic buildings, and as Eva Griffith writes in her study 'a place that must have been associated in many minds with the old forms of belief and worship' as well as with theatre, adds extra frisson to the devil's presence in this staged monastery.[20]

Dekker adapted his source-material in order to bring language to the fore of Rush's proprioceptive temptation. *If This Be Not a Good Play* draws on the late-medieval German folk myth of Bruder Rausch, or Friar Rush in English instantiations. This myth describes a devil who infiltrates a monastery in the guise of monk called Bruder Rausch. Bruder Rausch kills the monastery cook by boiling him in his own pan, then steadily rises through the monastery ranks. He incites the monks to sin by arranging for them to have sex with women, and by carving clubs which he leaves around the monastery prompting the monks to seize them and murder each other. Dekker's play appears to be the earliest extant English version of this story, though explicit references to Friar Rush in a variety of early modern texts (ranging from the mid-16th century *Gammer Gurton's Needle* to Reginald Scot's 1584 *Discoverie of Witchcraft*) and cultural activities such as Christmas games, as well as the influence of the plot in devil plays such as Christopher Marlowe's *Dr Faustus* (c. 1592), Ben Jonson's *The Devil Is an Ass* (1616) and *Grim the Collier of Croydon* (c. 1600, discussed in Chapter 4 of this book), show that the myth had been circulating in English culture for several decades by 1611.[21]

Mr S's Cambridge University play *Gammer Gurton's Needle* (first published 1575, performed some decades previously) suggests that the Friar Rush myth structured the ways in which people in early modern England visualised the devil. Claiming to have seen 'a great blacke devil', the character Hodge uses Friar Rush as the touchstone for his florid description:

> Gammer: But Hodge, had he no horns to pushe?
> Hodge: As long as your two arms, saw ye never Fryer Rushe
>   Painted on a cloth, with a wide long cowes tayle,
>   And crooked cloven feet, and many a hoked nayl? ...
>   Loke even what face Frier rush had, the devil had such another.[22]

Sixteenth and seventeenth century European (including English) woodcuts of Friar Rush show him goggle-eyed, claw-footed, fanged, and with a sizeable tail sweeping out from beneath his monk's habit.[23] *Gammer Gurton's Needle* suggests that Friar Rush appeared in the same way on painted cloths in early modern English homes or public spaces, thus Dekker could have borrowed aspects of this folkloric image to cue his audiences in to the visual shock of a devil saying grace, perhaps equipping his actor with a tail, long horns, and hooked nails to clash with his friar's garb. There may be some cross-pollination between stage and wider society here; the 'blacke devil' in Hodge's imagination may have stemmed from the blackened faces of early modern stage devils.[24]

Gammer Gurton's Needle is a play about a group of people searching for a needle, picking up unlikely objects in the false belief that they are the needle, and generally whipping each other into a frenzy with false stories like Hodge's supposed demonic encounter. *Gammer Gurton's Needle* has been read as an anti-Catholic satire; in this play, a stereotyped version of the Catholic belief that Eucharistic bread and wine are Christ's body and blood translates into a general incapacity accurately to perceive the world: a painted cloth is a devil, a straw looks like a needle. Frank Ardolino argues that the play pits Catholic 'misperception' against superior Protestant textual interpretation; Mr S depicts Catholic characters as overly enmeshed in the material world and constantly tricked by its false appearances.[25] By prompting his (officially at least) mainly Protestant audience kinaesthetically to imagine the monks' experiences of eating and drinking, Dekker's use of the Friar Rush myth blurs any simplistic distinction between Catholic materialism and abstract Protestant hermeneutics.

The linguist Robert Priebsch wrote, in the early twentieth century, the only currently available sustained study of Bruder Rausch. Priebsch suggests that pre-1620 Netherlandish printings of an anonymous comedic English prose text *The Historie of Frier Rush* (dated 1620 in its earliest English printing) may have influenced Dekker.[26] Priebsch argues that Dekker took the 'raw stones' ('die rohen Steine') from this prose story and turned them into his own 'broad building', though Priebsch is mixed in his praise of Dekker's 'skilful, unfortunately all-too-hastily-working hands'.[27] *The Historie of Frier Rush* sticks close to the German story, including with the detail of 'how Rush threw the maister Cooke into a kettell of water, seething vpon the fire, wherein he died'.[28]

Dekker's key alteration to this legend in all its forms is having his Friar Rush swap places with the cook not by killing him but by mis-saying grace so persuasively that Scumbroath amicably hands over his chef's role to Rush. Dekker's change is important because it changes the story to focus not on an insidious and comedically appropriate act of violence (killing the cook by cooking him in his own pan) but on grace, which is an act combining language, proprioception, and embodied imagination. Rush's language in the grace is at once richly corporeal and spiritually affecting. Onomatopoeic Middle German *ruschen* means to make a din, rustle, or whoosh, like wind. Dekker's Rush is a gust fanning a hot, destructive fire in body, mind, and soul. Later in the chapter, I will show how Dekker traces this intensifying somatic fire, but first it is worth dwelling on Rush's grace as a space that holds, and ultimately guides, the attention.

Dekker's friars initially reject Rush's grace. The Prior's main concern is perhaps the difference between the food the monks are eating and the food Rush has described: it amounts to discomfiting 'mock[ery]'. The Subprior pinpoints a deeper issue: such luxurious food would run contrary to the rules of their monastic order. Shacklesoul/Rush then invokes the idea of treason (something usually happening on a national level against a monarch) against an intimate bodily space (their stomachs). The word 'treason' positions the stomach, rather than the head or God, as king of the body:

> Prior: How dar'st thou mock us thou ill nurtur'd slave?
> Sub[prior]: Contemnst thou our order and religious fare?
> Shack: He has spoken treason to all our stomachs.[29]

Rush responds in mock contrition, as if he had genuinely thought that the monks would be eating the types of food outlined in his grace:

> Alas (my Lord) I thought it had bin here
> As in the neighbouring Churches, where the poor'st Vicar
> Is filled vp to the chin with choice of meates...[30]

'Filled vp to the chin with choice of meates', suggests the more common phrase 'filled up to the brim'; by replacing 'brim' with 'chin', Dekker constructs the body as a vessel to be filled. Dekker leaves room for a range of kinaesthetic understandings of this phrase. Being 'filled vp to the chin' perhaps suggests food guzzled faster than it can be swallowed or digested, backing up in the diner's oesophagus right up to their chin. Or it may suggest to you an eater whose full stomach bulges against their chin. Encountering the words 'up to the chin', readers might imagine their chin lifted by rising food or a rising belly. This phrase may also evoke an image of a person holding many dishes in their arms, piling them high, and using their chin to pin down and steady the teetering load. Later in this chapter, I will return to the rest of Rush's reply, which brings ideas of temperature and pampering into the mix. But let us move on to see how Rush drives home his emphasis on the body when he is made monastery cook, by appending a further list of foods to the menu he offered in his grace (including 'kick-choses', perhaps 'quelque-choses': 'things'):

> To *Scumbroath,* what I know ile teach,
> To make candels, Jellies, leach,
> Sirrup of violets, and of roses,
> Cow slip sallads, and kick-choses,
> Preserue the apricock, and cherry,
> Damsin, peare plom, raspis berry;
> Potates ike if you shall lack,
> To corroborate the back:
> A hundred more shall *Rush* deuice . . .[31]

This is a largely sugary counterpoint to the savouries Rush listed in the grace. When humans eat savoury food to satiety, we can often still find room for sweet dishes; Rush exploits this to augment the monks' greed. The monks may have thought their minds and bellies had expanded sufficiently, imagining themselves stuffed full with foods from the grace. Listening to Rush's list of education topics for Scumbroath, the monks discover more stomach-room and renewed desire to eat as they contemplate syrups, jellies, and preserves.

Dekker's devil holds our attention and visibly captures the monks' bodies and attentions. Usually, we might expect hungry diners' attention spans to wane as they listen to an overlong grace: they want grace to end so they can start on the food! In a comic twist, Rush's listeners onstage and off may well become increasingly rapt as his sizeable grace continues. The length of the grace itself intensifies the comedic effect as it allows for substantial stage business before the monks' explosive responses. Though no stage directions explicitly state that the actors would have shown signs of hunger, Rush gives them room to do so; these responses are perhaps so obvious that no stage directions are needed. The fact that the play is rarely or never performed nowadays and seems not to have been revived frequently (it was only published once, in 1612 quarto) entails that staging remains more of an imaginative exercise for modern readers; we might imagine the monks gaping or rubbing their stomachs, and assuming then forgetting a praying posture: initially clasping their hands then unclasping them, closing their eyes then opening them in amazement. Rush's long grace marks a time during which the devil acts on the monks' bodies, shaping the way they think and feel before launching them into the world to damn themselves.

As a demarcated stretch of time with a spiritual meaning, early modern grace was particularly charged for those possessed and influenced by devils. In an anonymous 1593 account, a child called Elizabeth Throckmorton supposedly bewitched by the devil in East England, was 'held' during grace:

> She continued well until night, and before Supper in time of thanksgiving, it used her very strangely, taking her at the very name of grace, and holding her no longer then grace was in saying: She sate very well at the Table, but no sooner had she put up her knife, but it pitched her backwards, then being taken from the table she was well until thanksgiving, all which time she was most grievously used and no longer.[32]

The leadup to grace sends Throckmorton's body 'pitching'; during grace, the devil takes control of her: she is 'used', 'taken' and 'held'. The pamphlet does not specify how the devil uses her, but it may be similar to her response to prayers, 'with such scriching and outcries, and vehement neesing, as that it terrified the whole company', or to hearing Bible verses when the devil rages for the duration and grows quiet when the book is closed.[33] Grace is a time of intense proprioception for Throckmorton; instead of focusing on the textures and tastes of her food, her experience is of her own bodily boundaries: itching, rasping, expelling air and sound. She sneezes (neeses) and scriches, which may mean she screeches or (as she does elsewhere) scratches herself and/or others. The devil is manifest through its effects on Throckmorton's body, and through peripheral clues such as the sound of it lapping milk in the child's stomach.

With devils embodied by actors, the theatre makes these processes of temptation visible. Marlowe's *Doctor Faustus* stages a devil enraged by grace, as Faustus and Mephistopheles, rendered invisible, haunt the Pope's banquet. In the A text of the play (1604), the Pope crosses himself as he tucks in, and in the B text (1616) Faustus complains 'How now? Must euery bit be spiced with a Crosse?' (whether the Pope is seasoning himself or his food with this cross is unclear), prompting Faustus physically to attack the Pope.[34] Marlowe's prose source, translator P. F.'s *The Historie of the damnable life and deserved death of Doctor John Faustus* (1592), which the play often follows very closely, states, 'as he sat at meat, the Pope would ever be blessing and crossing over his mouth, Faustus could suffer it no longer, but up with his fist and smote the Pope on the face'.[35] Dekker's Friar Rush does more than Marlowe's devils: Dekker both shows the devil as a separate being in dialogue with the monks, and represents him negating this separateness when he holds, uses, and possesses their attention, bodies, and reason.

Thomas Heywood includes a very similar long, rhyming, menu-like grace in his play, *A Pleasant Conceited Comedy, Wherein Is Shewed How a Man May Chuse a Good Wife From a Bad*, performed and published several times from its first performance in 1602 through to the 1630s. Dekker is possibly making an intertextual joke, making Rush's grace seem immediately ominous by drawing on the associations of such a grace with murder, lust, and wickedness already established by Heywood. In Heywood's play, the pedant Aminadab says grace at the protagonist Young Arthur's feast. Young Arthur is holding the feast to mock his wife prior to murdering her with a poisoned drink. Also present is Arthur's mistress, whom he aims to make his second wife after murdering his first. Heywood uses rhyme and a tempting 'proface' to awake his listeners' taste. Aminadab deploys the kind of *occupatio* that Rush later uses to invite listeners to fill in tantalising gaps in his description with greedy imaginative work: what might be the 'other meate thats in the house' for instance? Aminadab's pacier internal rhymes initially provide quicker satisfaction than Rush's more drawn-out couplets, before relaxing into a coupleted grace similar to Rush's, suggesting a move into expansiveness as the mealtime spread gets increasingly substantial:

> Gloria deo, *sirs* proface,
> Attend me now whilst *I* say grace.
> For bread and salt, for grapes and malt,
> For flesh and fish, and euery dish:
> Mutton and beefe, of all meates cheefe:
> For Cow-heels, chitterlings, tripes and sowse,
> And other meate thats in the house:
> For racks, for brests, for legges, for loines,
> For pies with raisons, and with proines:
> For fritters, pancakes, and for frayes,
> For venison pasties and minct pies:
> Sheephead and garlick, brawne and mustard,
> Wafers, spiced cakes, tart and custard,

> For capons, rabets, pigges and geese,
> For apples, carawaies and cheese:
> For all these and many moe,
> Benidicamus domino.[36]

In Heywood's grace, at least some of the food seems actually to have been present on the table; the characters discuss pies (plural) in the oven and roast meat so tempting that the knavish character Pipkin is scolded for picking at it before the meal. Preparing and eating this luscious feast absorbs the household's attentions, providing cover for Arthur's wicked purpose. In Dekker's play, by contrast, the whole point is that the feast is *not* present. Dekker rewrites Heywood's grace (either directly or via some other shared source) but repositions our gaze not on the food but on the embodied imaginative responses of the hungering monks. Unlike Heywood, Dekker makes the grace central to his plot, using it to spark contentious dialogue, and (as we shall see) wringing its ambiguous language for sinful potential. Heywood's characters do not comment on the grace, they simply say 'Amen' and start eating. Dekker's do not cease to comment on it, with words and bodily signs.

By taking control of grace itself, Dekker's devil is perfectly positioned to 'shackle' these monks' souls. Grace is usually a way of protecting the ritual of eating from the devil's destabilising influence. As Margaret Visser has noted, the fact that grace was repeated daily in a communal (e.g., family) setting made it ideal for (re)producing and consolidating social, familial, and religious norms and beliefs.[37] Thus, many early modern Christian graces reinforce a specific sectarian doctrine, allegiances to the monarch, and children's obedience to their parents.[38] Grace's crucial role makes a mis-said grace particularly well-placed for unknitting societal structures. Moreover, grace provided a protective boundary shielding the eater and their food, and the act of eating itself, from the devil. A mis-said grace thus exposes the eater to damnation, making the body's boundaries vulnerable to devilish ingress. The anonymous account of Throckmorton's possession makes her mouth hypervisible as an ill-guarded gateway to the interior of her body. As well as her involuntary sneezing and crying out, her mouth gaped open for long periods during which she couldn't shut it; she worried about toads entering through her mouth, and her family decided that the spirit must be 'a spirit of the ayre, entring by a breath'.[39]

Dekker extrapolates the negative effects of this break in the protective boundary around the friars' food. Rush follows his grace with a ridiculous argument peppered with non-sequiturs; the Prior's answers as he accepts Rush's pseudo-logic demonstrate that greed has weakened his reason. Deploying the form of a logical argument (*Sic Disputo . . . e Contra*) Rush states, 'He that eats not good meate is dambd: *Sic Disputo*| If he that feedes well hath a good soule, then *e Contra*| No, he that feedes ill, hath a bad and a poor soule'.[40] Perhaps anticipating the full state of his stomach rather than appraising the completeness of the argument, the Prior echoes Rush's ambiguous vocabulary, pronouncing this, 'A full and edifying argument'.[41] The Prior begins to think with his stomach; he has swallowed Rush's words. To the Subprior's outrage, the monks urge Scumbroath to learn from their new cook, Rush, by nightfall so that they can begin banqueting as soon as possible. Handing Rush complete control of their diet, they give him easy access to the interiors of their bodies.

A Gust of Wind That Fans the Fire – Monks Hotting Up

Dekker uses temperature vocabulary to track the intensifying effects of Rush's grace. Rush's vocabulary in the grace-scene confuses the bodily and the spiritual, allowing him to manipulate the monks' souls via their bodies. Rush invites the monks to imagine the feel of 'piping hot' meats on their lips and mouths, and settling warmingly into their stomachs; his words simultaneously have a warming, inflaming effect on their souls. As we have seen, Rush responds with feigned ingenuousness to the monks' initial indignation at his grace. Here is the quotation again, with more of Rush's tempting lies:

> Alas (my Lord) I thought it had bin here
> As in the neighbouring Churches, where the poor'st Vicar
> Is filled vp to the chin with choice of meates,
> Yet seekes new ways to whet dull appetite
> As there with holy spels mens soules they cherish,
> So with delitious fare, they themselues nourish.
> Nor want they argument for sweete belly-cheere.[42]

Rush's final half-rhyming couplet links religious prayers or rituals with delicious feasts. As he does throughout the play, Rush here exploits language that can refer to both morality and sensuality: 'cherish' could mean 'to pamper' but also 'to keep warm'; the parallelism 'as ... so' suggests that his piping hot meats will warm the body in a similar way to prayer (which he tellingly describes in an impiously occult manner as 'spels') warming the soul. 'Cherish' suggests that prayer might simply be a form of pampering, further weakening the boundary between bodily luxury and religious ritual. When, through polyptoton playing on a common meaning of 'to gladden', 'cherish' morphs into 'cheere' as part of the phrase 'belly-cheere', the sense of 'cherish' veers definitively towards the stomach rather than soul.

Rush's pseudo-logical argument explicitly links spiritual and physical heat, 'Sic probo: the soule followes the temperature of the body, hee that feedes well hath a good temperature of body, Ergo, he that feedes well hath a good soule'.[43] Rush exploits the common early modern Galenic idea that 'the soul follows the body's temperature': a hot body means a hot (angry, lustful, irritable) soul or mood.[44] The poet and cultural writer Richard Braithwaite's 'Of Sleepe', published 1619, states, 'Yet see we oft the *temper of the Soule| Follow the Bodies various temperature*'.[45] Within frameworks of humoral theory, some foods and drinks (like the beef in Rush's grace, and the alcohol the monks later drink) heated the body and brain while others cooled them.[46] Dekker is probably not asserting the indisputable truth of the notion that the soul always follows the body's temperature; the idea is simply useful for the argument he wants to make. Indeed, theologians and literary writers contested this notion, in texts with titles like 'The soule is ... more th[a]n a ... temperature of humours', or 'That the Soule Simpathiseth with the Body and Followeth her Crasis and Temperature'.[47] 'R. B.' (potentially Braithwaite again), author of a 1614 philosophical work, implicitly framed the issue as a choice between whether we allow the body or the soul to set our overall temperature, concluding, 'the body should take her temperature from the soule, and not the soule from the body.'[48] Dekker's monks teeter on the edge of this choice. The Subprior resists all Rush's assaults: the grace, beautiful apparitions designed to provoke lust, and death-threats. The other monks completely fail to resist. By staging these different outcomes, Dekker suggests that each monk's reaction to the grace is a matter of personal, spiritual responsibility, and that it *is* a choice.

Early modern graces often drew explicit parallels between physical and spiritual sustenance, with the ideal diner grateful for run-of-the-mill (pun intended) bread and Christ the spiritual Bread of Life.[49] The 1566 Catechism of the Council of Trent affirmed that though for Catholics transubstantiated bread and wine seem externally to be bread and wine, their substance has changed into Christ's body and blood. This Catechism states that though bodily nourishment can be a metaphor for spiritual nourishment, the Eucharist is food for the soul, 'For what bread and wine are to the body, the Eucharist is to the health and delight of the soul, but in a higher and better way'; moreover while in everyday eating our bodies change the food through digestion, the Eucharist changes *us*, 'this Sacrament is not, like bread and wine, changed into our substance; but we are, in some wise, changed into its nature'.[50] As we saw with Gammer Gurton's needle, several early modern English dramatists wilfully misunderstood and stereotyped these views, depicting Catholic characters as easily tricked into false beliefs that defy the evidence of the senses. Dekker falls into this category, representing a near-universal human condition (we salivate over descriptions of food when we are hungry) through a sectarian lens; with the exception of the Subprior, his monks' imaginations are easily manipulated by Rush's tempting menu.

Rush exploits grace's desirable links between the spiritual and sensual in three steps. First, he posits the holiness of greedy indulgence through his nourish/cherish conflation. Then, he distracts the monks from the spiritual consequences of their actions completely, goading them to immerse themselves in bodily pleasures and frustrations alone. Finally, he brings the monks abruptly back to the spiritual plane once they have damned themselves and are destined for hell. Rush's false equivalences encourage the monks to misread their own interoceptive and proprioceptive signals, mistaking the bodily warmth of a large hot meal and a lot of alcohol with the spiritual warmth of comforting faith and prayer. Conflating interpersonal and physical warmth may be a peculiarity of English; as the linguists Felix Ameka and Maria Koptjevskaja-Tamm show, other languages distinguish more finely between warm emotions and high temperatures.[51] If so, the English language works in Rush's favour. Physical warmth can be associated with qualities like comfort, sociability, generosity, and benevolence, but also negative emotions like fury or sinful lust.[52] Offering the monks the former group of experiences, Rush in fact serves them up the latter. In one soliloquy, Rush exposes his logic, 'Ingender sin with sin, that wines rich heate| May bring forth Lust, Lust murder may beget'.[53]

Rush seems regularly to take the monks' temperatures, noting with satisfaction that they get ever warmer with lust and rage until they are (he hopes) 'scalding' in hell. For example, when two monks fight to the death, Rush frames this as mere heat brought on by drunkenness; downplaying the murder in this way enables Rush to encourage the remaining monks to keep drinking. It is another illogical argument, but logic is all but dead in this monastery, with only the clear-headed Subprior to uphold it. Seeing the other monks running with spades and pruning knives to the vineyard, the Subprior rebukes them, reminding them that two drunken monks have recently killed each other:

> *Sub.* Your Vines?
> (The tree of sin and shame?) this Serpent here,
> Hee with that liquorish poison, so set on fire
> The braines of *Nicodeme* and *Siluester*,
> That they in drunken rage have stabd each other.[54]

Rush responds by playing down the dangers of drink and repositioning himself as the two monks' saviour rather than the instigator of their brawl:

> Yes, they bleede a little, but have no harme,
> Their yong blood with the grapes Iuice being made warme,
> They brawld and struck, but I kept off the blowes.[55]

The Subprior identifies a huge heat: the monks were 'set on fire'. Rush redescribes the fire as mere warmth, appropriate to young blood. Rush tries to convince the monks that (as the frogs tell themselves while letting themselves boil to death in the proverbial gradually-heating saucepan) their bodies are not so dangerously hot that they need to take drastic action to save themselves. Rush's harme/warme rhyme emphasises the link between harm and heat in this strand of the plot, but also denies it by transforming words. Perhaps he intends his listeners to think they misheard: the monks did not come to 'harme', they were simply 'warme'.

Towards the end of the play, describing how the bibulous Prior has choked to death on a grape kernel, Scumbroath focuses on the deceased man's gullet. Scumbroath's narration, shocking his interlocutor the Subprior, is apt to provoke irritating kinaesthetic responses with its emphasis on the sensitive inner skin of the throat 'choackt', 'stopt' with a kernel, poked with a stick, cut with a knife, and rummaged around in by Scumbroath's fingers. Any kinaesthetic relief we feel, living through this paragraph, as the throat is cut and the uncomfortable stone taken out, is simultaneously ruined by our knowledge that this is a deadly cut. Irritating for us to contemplate too, is Scumbroath's image of lips unlicked. Though Scumbroath is not ostensibly saying that the Prior resists licking his lips, by deploying this image and provoking us to imagine it kinaesthetically, he helps us to feel some of the Prior's frustration and inability to lift his mind from his body. Attempting not to lick our lips is difficult; we can grow frantic obsessing over how much we want to lick our dry lips and how much longer we can hold out:

Scum: Yes, choackt: that of which men die ore night, and are well the next morning, wine has kild the Lord Pryor: he woud in a brauerie taste the liquor of our Vines, because you threatened he should neuer licke his lippes after. And the Kernell of a grape stopt his windepipe, for want of a skowring-sticke.
Sub: Art thou sure hee is dead?
Scum: How dead, because I wud be sure, I cut his throate of purpose, to take out the Kernell.[56]

This blunt description of the mechanics of drinking, dying, and Scumbroath's botched first-aid-cum-murder pinpoints the throat as the site of sin and retribution. Harking too much to the gannet-like pleasures of feeling food and drink sliding down his throat leaves the Prior at his throat's mercy. He is unable to help himself when he chokes; the knife drawn across this part of the body sends his soul to hell.

Scumbroath is particularly susceptible to the rise in temperature Rush instigates. Angered by Rush's machinations, Scumbroath declares, 'Ile make him know what tis to boile a cooke in's own grease.| I am scalding hot ... I carie a heart-burning within me'.[57] It is a little unclear whom the cook in Scumbroath's threat is. In earlier stories, as we saw, Rush does boil the previous cook in his own pan so perhaps Scumbroath is experiencing this act in a metaphorical sense: though Rush does not literally cook Scumbroath in the kitchen, he makes Scumbroath so angry that Scumbroath's body fat sizzles. Or, because Rush is now the cook, is Scumbroath threatening to boil *Rush*, thereby enacting revenge on behalf of all Scumbroath's textual predecessors? The Subprior, the one monk Rush cannot tempt, as 'wines lustfull fires him warme not', has a momentary cooling effect on Scumbroath.[58] As the Subprior dissuades him from his plan to kill Rush, Scumbroath reflects that the Subprior's words cause his anger to subside, or to mingle with it as cold water swirls into scalding water, leaving it tepid (two possible meanings of 'laid'): 'the cold water of your counsel has laid the heate of my furie'.[59] Chancing upon Shacklesoul gloating with other devils about his success in the monastery and thereby realising that Rush is a devil in disguise, Scumbroath realises that his own hot anger harms others, 'The best is, if I be a match in the diuels tinderbox, I can stincke no worse than I doe alreadie'.[60] This image partly represents Scumbroath's insight into his own stench (which we imagine as sharp and sulphurous like a struck match) now that he has sunk into beggary after being demoted as cook. It simultaneously signals that, like a struck match ready to start a fire, Scumbroath's body has become a tool in another's hand able to do significant damage to his environment.

In the play's decidedly hot finale in hell, Scumbroath's 'heart burning' becomes painfully literal. The avaricious character Barterville, from another strand of the plot, feels his heart literally on fire and cries out among the damned tormented by extreme heat: 'it scaldes! it scaldes! it scaldes!'

Barterville:	Whooh: hot, hot, hot,-drinck,-I am heart-burnt.
Prodigall:	One drop, a bit.
Faulx:	Now, now, now.
Barterville:	I am perbold, I am stewd, I am sod in a kettle of brimstone, pottage—it scaldes,—it scaldes,—it scaldes,—it scaldes—whooh

Diuels:	Ha ha ha.
Prodigall:	But one halfe crom, a little little drop, a bit . . .
Omnes:	One drop of puddle water to coole vs.⁶¹

Like the biblical Dives, Dekker's damned (who include the real-life Guy Fawkes, 'Faulx') call for the merest water-drop but are denied (Luke 16:23–6). Dekker does not specify which if any of the monks are among the 'omnes' clamouring for cool water, however disgusting. However, it would fit the plot if (with the exception of the Subprior), all the monks are present in hell. Prodigall, a character introduced for the first time in this hell scene, may be present because of links in the early modern European Protestant imagination between unsaid grace and the Biblical prodigal son; prints depicted families that did not say grace properly together ending up broken, like the story of the prodigal son without its happy ending.⁶² This link may account for references to the prodigal son in *If This Be Not a Good Play* and *A Pleasant Conceited Comedy*, both plays featuring poorly- or un-said graces.⁶³

Bolens emphasises the instructional power of proprioceptive kinesic and kinaesthetic intelligence, particularly in the context of the Eucharist, wherein 'the body in its literality becomes the main expressive means of the soul; it symbolizes it and becomes its symptom'.⁶⁴ For Bolens, reflecting on proprioceptive experiences during communion could make early moderns more aware of their own processes of embodied understanding, and of the state of their souls; this 'complicates any effort to distinguish between the literal and the figural'.⁶⁵ This was part of the ways in which, more widely, early modern people relied on 'perceptual simulations' and kinesic intelligence to understand heavenly matters; Bolens gives the example of St Augustine using kinesic imagery of vessels being filled to the brim to help his reader understand heaven and earth's inability to contain God.⁶⁶ Though (as Bolens notes) early modern Protestants returned to 'a figural reading of the phenomenon' of transubstantiation, in what Gillian Woods calls 'unreformed fictions', with literary writers frequently returning to older Catholic images and metaphors.⁶⁷ As we have seen, early modern writers frequently understood saying grace as a way of recalling or referring to the Eucharist, and Dekker implicates the monks' act of saying grace in inflammatory stereotypes about materialist Catholic beliefs in transubstantiation. Though they are alert to their own heat, however, when Dekker's damned reach hell they fail spectacularly to learn anything spiritual from their painful feelings. Dekker's damned characters do not gain understanding but rather are stuck in a *realisation*: that their bodies are burning, that they want to alleviate the heat but cannot. Typically for what Griffith calls the 'noisy, spectacle driven kinds of drama' at the Red Bull, Dekker ends his play with yelling voices and spectacular heat: devils force-feed sinners molten gold and hot blood; one sinner (real-life committer of regicide Ravaillac) has his hand 'burnt off'.[68]

In *Dekker his Dreame* (1620), a poem describing a dream lasting seven years that includes a dream-journey into hell, Dekker personally experiences 'hels infinite *Heate*' as well as its infinite cold.[69] There, Lucifer sits on a burning throne; not pained by the heat, Lucifer glories in it. He is crowned with heat:

> The Prince of Darkenesse, sate upon a Thorne
> Of red-hot Steele, and on his head a Crowne
> Of Glowing Adamant: As in he drew
> The noisome Ayre, flames from his nostrils flew,
> His Eyes flash'd fire . . .[70]

Dekker His Dreame offers several similarities to *If This Be Not a Good Play*. Like Barterville who, true to his name, attempts to barter his way out of hell with his wealth, the damned in Dekker's dream 'offred worlds of *Treasure*' for 'One drop of *Water*' but are denied.[71] This poem is full of heat, from macro views of damned souls submerged in blazing brimstone and boiling blood, to the fine detail of the once-perfumed hair of courtiers in flames.[72] What is especially striking perhaps though, given the ominous overtones of heat in *If This Be Not a Good Play,* is that *Dekker His Dreame* describes Dekker's poetic inspiration itself in terms of heat.

The epigraph to *Dekker His Dreame*, a quotation from Ovid's *Fasti*, describes God moving in us thereby warming us with inspiration, 'Est Deus in Nobis, agitante calescimus illo'. Calescimus can mean both 'we grow hot' and 'we are inspired'; throughout *Dekker His Dreame* it is ambiguous which is which. The woodcut on the frontispiece depicts a person in a four poster bed, whom we might be expected to assume is Dekker. One arm lies outside the covers and the other props his head up. The curved lines in the bedclothes suggest linen scrunched by Dekker's rolling, curling and uncurling body. This woodcut might evoke tossing and turning heatedly in bed, throwing limbs out into the cool air, and the feverish dreams attendant on this uncomfortable situation. In his dedication to the (then rising) courtier Endymion Porter, Dekker describes his bed as unpleasant,

> the Bed on which seven years I lay Dreaming, was filled with thornes instead of fethers, my pillow a rugged flint, my Chamberfellowes (sorrowes that day and night kept me company) the very, or worse than the very Infernall Furies.[73]

Much of the poem's heat centres in Dekker's tormented eyes and brain:

> O my weake eyes! how did your *Balls* (me thought)
> Burne out their Ielly, when they had but caught
> One little-little glimpse of those *Diuine*
> And in-accessible *Beames,* which did out-shine
> Hot-glowing coales of *Fire?* no mortall *Sight*
> Can stand a *Maiesty* so infinite.[74]

In 'catching' [sic] a glimpse of God's 'Beames', Dekker's eyeballs 'catch' in a second sense of catching on fire. Dekker deploys somatic imagery of the eye's balls and jelly, tangible 'beames' and 'hot-glowing coales', yet also undermines it as the sight of God far exceeds these physical experiences. Though the heat burns away the jelly of Dekker's eyes and he cannot withstand it, he continues his vision. About a third of his section on the 'Horror of Hell Fire' is about how, despite his burnt-out eyes and 'weake Sight', Dekker can still see:

> My Spirit had balls of Wild-fire in his head
> For Eyes (me thought) and I by them was led:
> For All these coale-pits (faddom'd deepe as hell)
> Still burne, yet are the Flames Inuisible.[75]

This heat is resolutely textual. Only in a literary text can infinite heat burn away the jelly of a person's eyes and replace them with 'balls of Wild-fire' so that they can see and report on 'Flames Inuisible'. *If This Be Not a Good Play* represents a similar conundrum: the sinners burn perpetually yet (as they complain) they are never consumed by hell's fire. These literary texts offer readers the unique opportunity to experience something of hellfire and emerge unscathed. Neither reader nor author may wish to dwell there long; later in his *Dreame*, Dekker leaves hell 'on wings of hot desire', ready to record his journey with heated description.[76]

Mistrusting the Self

The monks in *If This Be Not a Good Play* are challenged to believe their greedy imaginations rather than their eyes or moral compasses. Dekker's comedy may be drawing on Eucharistic debates about (dis)trusting our senses when it comes to transubstantiated food. According to the Council of Trent, though transubstantiated Eucharistic bread and wine may taste, smell and feel like bread and wine, its substance instantly changes at the moment of transubstantiation into Christ's body and blood. Listing his various salads and desserts, as I quoted above, Rush promises,

> A hundred more shall *Rush* deuice,
> And yet to early mattins rise,
> Our ladies office, sing at prime,
> At euen-song, and at compline time.
> Chant Anthems, Aniuersaries, Dirges,
> And the dolefull *de profundis*.[77]

Rush's statement that despite preparing over 'a hundred' delectable dishes he will still have time to rise early for matins and fulfil all his duties of singing and chanting throughout the day suggests that he will conjure up these dishes very quickly indeed, even instantaneously. He is perhaps even quicker than the Rush in the 1620 prose *Historie* who is 'very quicke in his office' at cooking half a cow for dinner when he returns late to the monastery one afternoon.[78] This hints not at normal cookery but diabolical conjuration.

Thomas Heywood and Richard Brome's *The Late Lancashire Witches* (1634), like *If This Be Not a Good Play*, describes a diabolically-transformed meal with loaded vocabulary that suggests a devilish version of transubstantiation. In *The Late Lancashire Witches*, the eponymous witches bewitch the Seely household, controlling everything from the family members' relationships with each other to the food they eat. The speed with which the witches transform a meat-based meal into unappetising food is one of the key signs that diabolical magic is involved. Seely proudly reads the planned menu for the guests, probably unrolling a stage-scroll or producing a document as Rush does to read his grace,

> 'Tis a busie time, yet will I review the Bill of fare, for this dayes dinner— (Reades) for 40· people of the best quality, 4. messes of meat; viz. a leg of Mutton in plum-broth, a dish of Marrowbones, a white-broth, a Surlovne of beefe, a Pig, a Goose, a Turkie, and two Pyes: for the second course, to every messe 4. Chickens in a dish, a couple of Rabbets, Custard, Flawn, Florentines, and stewd pruines,—all very good Country fare.[79]

The witches transform this banquet into a selection of mushroom salads (including puffballs or 'Puck fists' and 'Jew's Ears', a still-used English name for the *A. auricula judae* mushroom, showing the continued anti-semitism in today's society), insects and other critters, and cow dung or 'sheards'. Seely's wife Joan runs in exclaiming that there has been a mishap ('chance'):

> O husband, O guests, O sonne, O Gentlemen, such a chance in a Kitchin was never heard of, all the meat is flowne out o' the chimney top I thinke, and nothing instead of it, but Snakes, Bats, Frogs, Beetles, Hornets, and Humble-bees; all the Sallets are turn'd to Iewes-eares, Mushromes, and Puck fists; and all the Custards into Cow sheards! . . .[80]

One of the key surprises of Heywood and Brome's wedding feast is the difference between the expected taste and texture of the food (as advertised by Seely in his menu) and the actual taste and texture: cow dung, wiggling insects, clammy frogs, and mushrooms. It is obvious to the eaters' senses that their food is bewitched.

This marked change in the food can be read alongside ideas about the Eucharist. Early modern people who expressed disbelief in transubstantiation often did so by stating that the bread and wine looked, felt, and tasted the same before and after it had been transubstantiated. Bodleian MS Eng 2774, a collection of seventeenth-century sermons and sermon notes, returns repeatedly to this idea; 'all the senses shall tell us, that we tast nothing but bread, we se nothing but bread, we touch nothing but bread, and eat nothing but bread. When every sense (I say) makes it evident that it is bread, why should we say, it is the body of Ch. when it is nothing els but bread'.[81] For those who believed in transubstantiation, this did not seem to be a problem: indeed, it was part of the deep mystery of transubstantiation that the bread and wine appeared 'externally' in taste, texture, and scent, to be ordinary food and yet in fact were the body and blood of Christ. In *The Late Lancashire Witches*, where no grace is said, the feast undergoes a devilishly obvious transformation, the extravagant obverse of the indetectable transubstantiation posited by authors such as the sermon-writer just cited.

Confronted with transubstantiated bread and wine, worshippers might ask themselves whether they trust their senses, or their faith. Confronted with an entirely imaginary meal, Dekker's monks trust to tempting language, coaxed onwards by their hungry bodily responses. Presented with the transformed feast, Arthur in *The Late Lancashire Witches* boasts, 'I defie all Witches, and all their workes; their power on our meat, cannot reach our persons'.[82] Reading this play alongside Dekker's suggests that Arthur is in more danger than he allows himself to appreciate. As we saw, it is precisely his power over the monks' meat and his manipulation of culinary vocabulary that gives Rush 'power over [the monks'] persons'.

Conclusion

This chapter analysed the ways in which Friar Rush spread bad behaviour in a monastery. He did so by manipulating saying grace to provoke a range of kinaesthetic effects, stirring the monks' bodies from the inner juices of their stomachs to their chins. Dekker traces Rush's effect on the monastery through vocabulary of heat as the monks' blood 'warmed'.

Rush's effect further manifested in small kinaesthetic experiences that often existed only in the imagination: throats poked, stomachs bulging and warm, lips not licked but wet with inflaming wine. This play provokes such responses in readers and audiences but it is also *about* how language can provoke these responses and how dangerous this is.

Rush is well aware of what he is doing, taking control over the monks' meal enables him to bring in sins that 'shake' the fabric of society. Soliloquising after the grace scene, he recites a menu of sin. The rhyming coupleted list-like structure of this catalogue of sins echoes Shacklesoul's lists of delicious foods in the same scene, suggesting that each 'tempting dish' he has promised comes with extra helpings of hell:

> Charity: shees undon:
> Fat gluttony broke her back: next her step'd in
> Contention (who shakes Churches) now the sweete sin
> (Sallow lechery), should march after: Avarice,
> Murder, and all sinnes els, hell can device,
> Ile broach: the head's in, draw the body after,
> Begin thy feast in full cuppes, and end in slaughter.[83]

The 'sweet' taste the monks experience is in fact the taste of sin as the sensual experience of an improper feast slides into eschatological and moral territory: 'Begin thy feast in full cuppes, and end in slaughter'.

Rush's menu of sin draws attention to the gait. His enjambment reflects the way in which the sins step through the boundaries between the monastery, the monks' stomachs, hell, and the wider world. He presents their entry as a reversal of both birth and absolution, casting himself as a midwife-cum-anti-confessor pulling sins into the body rather than drawing them out: 'the head's in, draw the body after'. In imagining personified sins 'stepp[ing]' and 'march[ing]', he touches on the transgressive quality of the gait: the central topic of the next chapter. In the phrase 'the head's in, draw the body after', we do not know for sure if this wicked child is being pulled into or out of the body. Thus, we do not know whether the legs are coming first, or last. In the next chapter, as we shall see, in a late-sixteenth-early-seventeenth-century Spanish text and its 1622 English translation, the legs certainly come first.

Notes

1. See Eva Griffith, *A Jacobean Company and Its Playhouse: The Queen's Servants at the Red Bull Theatre (c.1605–1619)* (Cambridge: Cambridge University Press, 2013), 17; Marta Straznicky, 'The Red Bull Repertory in

Print 1605–60', *Early Theatre* 9(2) (2006), 144–56. Straznicky argues that the printed texts of Red Bull plays are attempts to document performance rather than supplant it.
2. Thomas Dekker, *If It Be Not Good, The Diuel Is In It* (London: for I. T., 1612), C4r. Copy in Bodleian archive; frontispiece lacking a printed date but bearing a handwritten '1613'; dated 1612 in online records. In the main body of this chapter, I use Dekker's alternative title from the playtext's running header, in which the joke seems clearer.
3. Earlier versions of some of the research behind this chapter are Laura Seymour 'The Feasting Table as the Gateway to Hell on the Early Modern Stage and Page', *Renaissance Studies* 34(3) (2020), 392–411; 'The Taste of Food in Hell: Cognition and the Buried Myth of Tantalus in Early Modern English Texts', in *The Literature of Hell* ed. Margaret Kean (Oxford: Boydell and Brewer, 2021), 77–102.
4. There is an extensive humanist tradition of depicting monks and nuns indulging in the pleasures of the flesh. In several cases such as Desiderius Erasmus' discussion of monks' attitudes in *The Godly Feast* (1522), the various pleasures of a meal (for instance, its taste, the opportunity to rest while one eats) are, when experienced correctly, desirable both for monks and lay people. Other depictions are more complex, like the monks in François Rabelais' *Gargantua* and *Pantagruel* (1532–1564); a key example is Frère Jean, who stands out from his more purely sinful brethren because he combines drunkenness and gourmandising with leanness, physical attractiveness and strength, charm, excellent knowledge of scripture, and super-human feats of violence. Dekker's more two-dimensional depiction of greedy monks bears more relation to crude anti-clerical satire in Protestant visual and textual traditions.
5. Dekker, *If It Be Not Good*, C3v.
6. Dekker, *If It Be Not Good*, C4r.
7. Dekker, *If It Be Not Good*, C4r.
8. 'She's neither fish nor flesh, a man knows not where to have her', William Shakespeare, *Henry IV* 3.3.122, in G. Blakemore Evans, Herschel Baker, and Anne Barton, eds, *The Riverside Shakespeare* (New York: Houghton Mifflin, 1996). Unless otherwise specified, all references to Shakespeare's works are to this edition. I am very grateful to Lorna Hutson for this reference. As well as suggesting sexual ambiguity, not being able to distinguish between flesh and fish would make it difficult for an early modern Catholic to know if they were following Christian dietary laws correctly on days when fish was a permitted foodstuff but flesh (other meats) were prohibited.
9. Ellen Spolsky, 'Elaborated Knowledge: Reading Kinesis in Pictures', *Poetics Today* 17(2) (1996) (pp. 157–80), 157.
10. Lucy Munro, 'Staging Taste', in Simon Smith, Amy Kenney, and Jacqueline Watson, eds, *The Senses in Early Modern England 1558–1660* (Manchester: Manchester University Press, 2015) (19–38), 20, and passim.
11. Dekker, *If It Be Not Good*, C4r.
12. On double prefixes and documents, see Tiffany Stern, *Documents of Performance in Early Modern England* (Cambridge: Cambridge University Press, 2009), 180–1; for texts onstage more generally, including menus and scrolls, see ibid., 174–200.

13. Cf. Thomas Nashe, *Have with You to Saffron Walden* (London: John Danter, 1596), I1r-v. I am very grateful to Lorna Hutson for this reference.
14. OED 'piping-hot', *adj.* C1 *a* and *b*.
15. Timothy Kendall, *Flowers of Epigrammes* (London: John Kingston, 1577), R7r. Several religious texts explain that if Christians do not acknowledge thankfully before eating that it is God who has allowed them to consume animals, they become no better than the animals themselves. 'I have seldome observed God served at the tables, eyther of Masters or men, by saying Grace and Thanksgiving, when like Hogges and Dogges they have served themselves with the usurped Creatures', writes Church of England clergyman Stephen Jerome, *Seven Helpes to Heaven Showing* (London: T Snodham, 1614), P3v.
16. Dekker, *If It Be Not Good*, B2r.
17. Dekker, *If It Be Not Good*, B2r.
18. Dekker, *If It Be Not Good*, B3r.
19. He is both 'Shac'/'Shak' and 'Rush' at Dekker, *If It Be Not Good*, C4r, for example.
20. Griffith, *A Jacobean Company and Its Playhouse*, 29.
21. This myth, first published in Germany in 1488 as *Broder Rusche* was probably of older, oral, origin. Robert Priebsch relates that 'Friar Rush' was the name of an early modern Christmas game, and may also have influenced the folkloric character Friar Tuck, *Bruder Rausch* (Zwickau: Ullmann, 1919), 45.
22. Mr S[tephenson], *A ryght pithy, pleasaunt and merie comedie, intytuled Gammer Gurton's Needle* (London: Thomas Colwell, 1575), C2v. I am very grateful for Lorna Hutson for directing me to focus on this passage. See Lorna Hutson, 'Theatre', in James Simpson and Brian Cummings, eds, *Cultural Reformation: Medieval and Renaissance in Literary History* (Oxford: Oxford University Press, 2018), 227–46. As Hutson explains, the play was performed 1553–4 or 1559–60 at Christ's College Cambridge (238).
23. For examples of woodcuts see Priebsch, 1919; Anon, *The Historie of Frier Rush* (London: Edward Allde, 1620), passim.
24. On the racism of this tradition, see Matthieu Chapman, *Anti-Black Racism in Early Modern English Drama: The Other "Other"* (London: Routledge, 2016), 26, 47; Robert Hornback, 'The Folly of Racism: Enslaving Blackness and the "Natural" Fool Tradition', *Medieval and Renaissance Drama in England* (20) (2007), 46–84. On cosmetics and fabrics used to blacken skin, see Ian Smith, 'White Skin, Black Masks: Racial Cross-Dressing on the Early Modern Stage', *Renaissance Drama* 32 (2003) (33–67), 51–2.
25. Frank Ardolino, 'Misperception and Protestant Reading in *Gammer Gurton's Needle*', *SEL* 50(1) (2010) (17–34), 24–29.
26. Anon, *The Historie of Frier Rush*, A2r-B1v.
27. 'Doch hat sie ihm nur die rohen Steine—und sie nicht einmal alle—geliefert, die unter den geschickten, leider nur allzu hastig arbeitenden Haenden des elisabethanischen Dramatikers zu einen weiten Bau emporgewachsen sind', Priebsch, *Bruder Rausch*, 46. Priebsch discusses it further at 66–7. The translation in the main body of the text is mine.
28. Anon, *The Historie of Frier Rush* (London: Edward Allde, 1620), A4v.

29. Dekker, *If It Be Not Good*, C4v.
30. Dekker, *If It Be Not Good*, C4v.
31. Dekker, *If It Be Not Good*, D2r.
32. Anon, *The Most Strange and admirable discoverie of the three witches of Warboys* (London: the Widdowe Orwin, 1593), B3v.
33. Anon, *The Most Strange and admirable discoverie*, B3v.
34. Cf Christopher Marlowe, *The Tragicall History of D. Faustus* (London: V.S., 1604), D2r; Christopher Marlowe, *The Tragicall History of the life and death of Doctor Faustus* (London: for John Wright, 1616), E1r.
35. P. F., trans, *The Historie of the damnable life and deserved death of Doctor John Faustus* (London: Thomas Orwin, 1592), C4r. 'Spiced' combines culinary and moral ideas; at the time it could signify 'seasoned' but also 'altered in character' and 'over-scrupulous of conscience' OED 'spice', *v* 1a-b; 'spiced' *adj.* 1a, 2a [accessed 21.07.2020].
36. Thomas Heywood, *A Pleasant Conceited Comedy* (London: for Matthew Lawe, 1602), G1v.
37. Margaret Visser, *The Rituals of Dinner* (London: Penguin, 2017 [1991]), 27.
38. For examples of early modern graces, see Henry Dixon, *Saying Grace Historically Considered* (Oxford: James Parker & Co, 1903), 141. For the pedagogical importance of saying grace, see e.g., Wayne Franits, 'The Family Saying Grace: A Theme in Dutch Art', *Simiolus* 16(1) (1986), 36–49.
39. Anon, B4v. For the devil entering the body through the mouth, see Philip Almond, *Demonic Possession and Exorcism in Early Modern England* (Cambridge: Cambridge University Press, 2004), 20. Gregory the Great provides an early example (a nun eating a lettuce with the devil inside, becoming possessed when she forgets to bless the lettuce or say grace), *Dialogues*, trans. Odo Zimmermann (Washington, DC: Catholic University of America Press, 2002 [1959]), 18.
40. Dekker, *If It Be Not Good*, D1r.
41. Dekker, *If It Be Not Good*, D1r.
42. Dekker, *If It Be Not Good*, C4v.
43. Dekker, *If It Be Not Good*, D1r.
44. Michael Schoenfeldt, *Bodies and Selves in Early Modern England* (Cambridge: Cambridge University Press, 1999), 9–12. For discussion see e.g., Gail Kern Paster, *Humoring the Body* (Chicago: Chicago University Press, 2004), 87.
45. Richard Braithwaite, *A New Spring* (London: G Eld, 1619), D3r.
46. For hot foods causing angry fantasies, see e.g., 'Gonzalo', *The Divine Dreamer* (London: sn, 1641), B1r, B2r. Schoenfeldt provides examples of other texts using similar wording to Dekker's, *Bodies and Selves*, 9–12.
47. John Davies, *A work for none but angels and men* (London: MS, 1653), frontispiece has the subtitle, 'the soule is . . . more th[a]n a . . . temperature of humours'; Thomas Walkingkton, 'That the Soule Simpathiseth with the Body and Followeth her Crasis and Temperature', in *The optick glasse of humors* (London: John Windet, 1607), C1v-C8v. For further discussion, see John Jackson, *The Soule is Immortall* (London: W. W., 1611), A4r.
48. R. B., *The Yong Mans Gleanings* (London: John Beale, 1614), E2r. For

discussion see e.g., Thomas Cooper, *The mystery of the holy government of our affections* (London: Bernard Alsop, 1620), B12r-v, John Harris, *The Divine Physician* (London: Nath Brook and Will Whitford, 1676), H8r.
49. A good example is Henry Bull's nearly two-decades-posthumously-published *Christian Prayers and Meditations* (London: R. Robinson, 1596), Z1r. Dixon's *Saying Grace Historically Considered* lists further examples, spanning centuries.
50. Pope Pius V, The Catechism of the Council of Trent, trans John McHugh and Charles Callan (Charlotte, NC: TAN Books, 1992 [first published 1923]), 158
51. Maria Koptjevskaja-Tamm, 'Introduction' in Maria Koptjevskaja-Tamm, ed, *The Linguistics of Temperature* (John Benjamins, 2015), 16–17. Felix Ameka explains that in Ewe, for example, generosity, comfort, and sociability are instead expressed through vocabulary of coldness, 'Hard Sun, Hot Weather, Skin Pain: The Cultural Semiotics of Temperature Experiences in Ewe and Lipke (West Africa)', *The Linguistics of Temperature*, 58–9. On examples of cultural factors affecting such slippages see Katarina Rasculić 'What's Hot and What's Not in English and Serbian', in *The Linguistics of Temperature*, 277, 294. For a useful further study of the complexities of temperature vocabulary in contemporary English see Gregorz Kleparski, 'Hot Pants, Cold Fish, and Cool Customers', *Studia Anglica Resoviensia* 4(47) (2007), 100–18.
52. For cognitive discussions of the effects of physical warmth on thoughts and emotions, and vice versa, see for example Laurence Williams and John Bargh, 'Experiencing Physical Warmth Promotes Interpersonal Warmth', *Science* 332 (2008), 606–7; Emma Firestone 'Warmth and Affection in *Henry IV*: Why No One Likes Prince Hal' in *Embodied Cognition and Shakespeare's Theatre: The Early Modern Body-Mind*, eds Laurie Johnson, John Sutton, and Evelyn Tribble (London: Routledge, 2014).
53. Dekker, *If It Be Not Good*, F3v.
54. Dekker, *If It Be Not Good*, F2v.
55. Dekker, *If It Be Not Good*, F2v.
56. Dekker, *If It Be Not Good*, K4v.
57. Dekker, *If It Be Not Good*, G1r.
58. Dekker, *If It Be Not Good*, F3v.
59. Dekker, *If It Be Not Good*, G1v.
60. Dekker, *If It Be Not Good*, I1r.
61. Dekker, *If It Be Not Good*, L3r-v. For discussion of this scene, see Seymour, 'The Taste of Food in Hell', 85–95.
62. Pieter van Thiel, '"Poor Parents, Rich Children" and "Family Saying Grace"', *Simiolus* 17(2/3) (1987), 90–149.
63. Scumbroath becomes 'the prodigall child in the painted cloth' (Dekker, *If It Be Not Good*, H4v). Young Arthur's father disowns him for being 'a spend-thrift, prodigall' (Heywood, *A Pleasant Conceited Comedy*, C1r).
64. Bolens, *The Style of Gestures*, 69.
65. Bolens, *The Style of Gestures*, 70.
66. Bolens, *The Style of Gestures*, 68.
67. Bolens, *The Style of Gestures*, 73; Gillian Woods, *Shakespeare's Unreformed Fictions* (Oxford: Oxford University Press, 2013).

68. Griffith, *A Jacobean Company and Its Playhouse*, 16; Dekker, *If It Be Not Good*, L4r.
69. Thomas Dekker, *Dekker His Dreame* (London, 1620), E3v.
70. Dekker, *Dekker His Dreame*, D2r.
71. Dekker, *Dekker His Dreame*, E3v.
72. Dekker, *Dekker His Dreame*, D1v.
73. Dekker, *Dekker His Dreame*, A2r.
74. Dekker, *Dekker His Dreame*, B4v.
75. Dekker, *Dekker His Dreame*, D3v.
76. Dekker, *Dekker His Dreame*, D3r.
77. Dekker, *If It Be Not Good*, D2r.
78. Anon, *The Historie of Frier Rush*, C3r.
79. Thomas Heywood and Richard Brome, *The Late Lancashire Witches* (London: Thomas Harper, 1634), E4r.
80. Heywood and Brome, *The Late Lancashire Witches*, E4v.
81. Anon, MS Eng 2774, Bodleian Library Oxford, fol 126r.
82. Heywood and Brome, *The Late Lancashire Witches*, E4v.
83. Dekker, *If It Be Not Good*, D3r.

Chapter 2

Walking Without God – (Mis)Learning Through the Gait in Mateo Alemán's *Guzmán de Alfarache* (1599 and 1604) and James Mabbe's *The Rogue* (1622)

In sixteenth-century Spain, a young man uses a church as his catwalk. Finely dressed but with his teeth loose from beatings sustained when he first set out into the violent and mendacious world, this young man, Guzmán, is especially proud of his stockings, garters, and Tudescan (-style) shoe fastenings. As he walks, therefore, Guzmán calls his readers', and other characters', attention to his legs: stretching, poising, and stiffening them. He struts like a chicken round and round the church, paying a visit to all its side-chapels; his purpose is not to pray but to gain maximum exposure for his flashily-clothed body. Guzmán's contrived gait garners plenty of attention from other worshippers, though not the adulatory kind he seeks and envisages. Guzmán recounts,

> I woke early on the Sunday. I got myself up looking fine, and hit the Great Church with vim and vigour. I went to hear Mass, though I suspect that I was more keen to be seen; I traversed the whole place three or four times and visited the chapels where more people were gathered until I came to idle among the choirs where there were many ladies and gallants. But I saw myself as the king of the cockerels, the one who'd won the prize, and like the lusty shepherd I showed off all my outfit, wanting them to see me and to remark on everything right up to the Tudescan fastenings. I stretched out my neck and began to inflate my belly and stiffen my legs: I was so vain about my looks and wiggling movements that everyone had to note me, laughing at my infamy. But however much they looked at me I didn't look into the matter nor did I examine my faults which were the cause of their laughs. Before now it seemed to me that they were admiring my curiosity and gallantry.
>
> Amaneció el domingo. Púseme de ostentación, y di de golpe con mi lozanía en la Iglesia Mayor, para oír misa, aunque sospecho que más me llevó la gana de ser mirado; paseéla toda tres o cuatro veces, visité las capillas donde acudía más gente, hasta que vine a parar entre los dos coros, donde estaban muchas damas y galanes. Pero yo me figuré que era el rey de los gallos y el que llevaba la gala, y como pastor lozano, hice plaza de todo el vestido, deseando que me

vieran y enseñar aun hasta las cintas, que eran del tudesco. Estiréme de cuello, comencé a hinchar la barriga, y atiesar las piernas. Tanto me desvanecía que de mis visajes y meneos todos tenían que notar, burlándose de mi necedad; mas como me miraban, yo no miraba en ello ni echaba de ver mis faltas, que era de lo que los otros formaban risas. Antes me pareció que los admiraba mi curiosidad y gallardía.[1]

Walking is the means through which Guzmán shapes and displays himself. More than this, at several crucial points in his life Guzmán learns through walking to be a rogue; through walking, too, he elicits and attempts to understand other people's appraisals of him. Through defiant walking and supine refusals to walk, he simultaneously resists learning, refusing to learn the lessons his society tries to teach him about the dangers of vanity and the virtues of Christian humility. This chapter examines the ways in which kinesic and kinaesthetic learning (as Guzmán's body teaches him through his gait) are curiously mixed with walking as a site of resistance to learning and change. Guzmán confronts and challenges the theories of generative, responsive kinesic and kinaesthetic learning I defined in the Introduction. As I explain below, central to my analysis is an examination of how Guzmán's walking, described in fictional prose, is a text that 'takes us for a walk'. Stylistically, the prose offers its own stumbles and limber jointedness; it extends stiffly, bends and wobbles.

This episode in the church occurs relatively early in the first part of the two-part picaresque novel *Guzmán de Alfarache* (part 1: Madrid, 1599; part 2 Lisbon, 1604), by Mateo Alemán y del Nero (1547–c. 1615). *Guzmán* describes how Guzmán from the town of Alfarache became a rogue (pícaro). Alemán was potentially a man of converso heritage; that is, his near ancestors may have been Jews forced to convert, or punished for not converting, to Catholicism by the Spanish Inquisition in the sixteenth century. Alemán writes two of his protagonists, the strutting Guzmán and his father, recognisably as conversos. *Guzmán* is narrated by the elder Guzmán, now enslaved in a galley, ostensibly looking back on his life with sober Christian conscience. However, the above-quoted passage is a prime example of how, when the Guzmán-narrator looks back on his younger self, he slips into celebrating rather than regretting his past behaviour. 'Meneos', Guzmán's movements in church, are wags, sways, and wiggles; 'meneos' could also mean business negotiations. Guzmán negotiates space and others' gazes with his body; it is a currency he hopes to exchange for social recognition. In modern times, especially in the world of music videos and lyrics, 'menear' is suggestively to wiggle one's hips and bum. Guzmán is 'rude' in the sense of being proud and arrogant, acting inappropriately for a formal religious setting, but equally in the sense of being filled with vigorous high spirits; 'lozanía' (which, for ease of initial understanding, I translated as 'vim and vigour' above) captures both these meanings. In this chapter, I argue that Guzmán's walking body asserts a kinesic power that resists any simplistic Christian narrative trajectory within the book. Like a bright light persisting in one's field of vision, the joyful image of Guzmán sashaying through the church is able to override any moral message about the vanity of his gait.

At various points in *Guzmán de Alfarache*, Guzmán's gait is a site of learning through mimicry that actually becomes resistance to socially- and religiously-acceptable learning. Strikingly, these moments tend to be crucial landmarks for his development as a rogue, prompting explicit reflections on how his deceitfulness has improved, and how he relates to others in society and to God and religious norms. The models Guzmán chooses to emulate are responsible for his increasingly 'bad' behaviour. He initially copies his wiggling strut and accompanying outfit from a gallant in Toledo; later, a beggar and his rulebook to display his legs to attract alms; later still, a satirical conduct book, the 'Arancel de Necedades', offers dire threats for minor infractions against good walking. In so doing, he engages in the kinaesthetic and kinesic learning Bolens describes: attempting to gain new outlooks, modes of being, and thought-patterns by imitating another person's bodily movements.[2] Guzmán's own body teaches him; when he is beaten and thoroughly tricked after advertising his naïveté in the church strut, his body seems to remember the adverse consequences of a strutting gait. As we shall see, when Guzmán begins to strut again in the second part of the novel, the activities of stretching, stiffening, and puffing-out seem to activate a muscle memory that warns him to take care.

As my previous chapter discussed with reference to Dekker's *If This Be Not a Good Play*, early modern texts have their own, specifically linguistic, kinaesthetic effects. Whenever Alemán describes Guzmán walking, the kinaesthetic melody of his prose evokes the rhythm of Guzmán's gait and draws our gaze up and down Guzmán's body (just as Guzmán desires!), resting on specific body parts. Describing the church strut, Alemán's linked clauses stop and start jerkingly with the sudden introduction of new verbs, evoking the oddly granular kinaesthetic melody and kinesic style of Guzmán's gait, 'Estiréme de cuello, comencé a hinchar la barriga, y atiesar las piernas' ('I stretched out my neck, began to inflate my belly, and stiffen my legs'). Jarringly, each body part seems consciously positioned, stiffened, or inflated, rather than working with the others as a harmonious whole. Circling within the church, Guzmán aims to showcase his style of walking rather than to reach a particular destination. The prose leads our gaze from his stretched neck to his swollen belly to his stiffened legs. This downward sweep of our (minds') eyes and the implied accompanying downwardly-curving motion of our neck, construct us as onlookers bowing humbly before Guzmán. Simultaneously, because each body part that the prose brings to our attention is itself engaged in outward movement, Guzmán expands to take up increasing space in our imagination. Led by the prose, our gaze follows Guzmán's corporeal expansion, travelling along his neck, outwards with his swollen belly and up and around the bulging muscles of his stiffened legs. Because of these kinesic effects, Guzmán's proud body looms large; because it has so persuasively engaged our own kinesic responses, Guzmán's body can be much more impressive than his snippy follow up moral statements about 'mis faltas' ('my faults').

Walking's rich metaphoricity for Alemán places the individual gait in wider terms of life as a journey, and incorporates the text itself. Alemán's textual gaits work within an established early modern and neoclassical tradition of seeing a sentence as travelling, the length and ligatures of its clauses determining its gait.[3] Aristotle's *Rhetoric* 3.9.6 expresses good prose speaking style as smooth walking,

> neither clauses nor periods should be curtailed or too long. If too short, they often make the hearer stumble; for when he is hurrying on towards the measure of which he already has a definite idea, if he is checked by the speaker stopping, a sort of stumble is bound to occur in consequence of the sudden stop. If too long, they leave the hearer behind, as those who do not turn till past the ordinary limit leave behind those who are walking with them.[4]

Aristotle exploits the fact that the Greek noun 'periodos' can mean 'march' as well as 'period' or 'clause'. For Aristotle, hearer and clause are closely tied; a 'sudden stop' in the speaker's patrol of words results in the hearer stopping suddenly, their stumbling (prosptaisis). As we 'walk with' Alemán's textual rhythms, his clauses ask us to stretch with Guzmán's legs, stop abruptly when Guzmán does, and to journey with Guzmán across Europe and North Africa and metaphorically towards or away from God. Alemán textualises the rhythms of Guzmán's gait; reading the text engages the reader's kinaesthetic experiences of stiffening, stretching, and forward motion to understand Guzmán's actions.

Spolsky argues that creating, reading, and interpreting a text is like an automatic capacity to walk; our ability to keep 'multiple and competing interpretations' in balance is like the ability to keep the body in balance when walking on uneven ground.[5] Spolsky offers her argument as an analogy between walking and reading. Because the vestibular system literally helps us both to walk and to read by stabilising our body and field of vision during both activities, I find that Spolsky's argument hovers richly over metaphorical and literally embodied ideas of 'balance' in interpretation. Spolsky writes,

> like one's trust that the ground you step on will not disappear before you take your next step, it is not something even philosophers pay regular attention to. And speaking of taking steps, I'd claim that the flexibility of language—the flexibility that allows users of words on a daily basis, and a fortiori allows creative artists to wry them, to swerve them as they attempt to communicate a new, personal understanding, to add a new perspective or emotional coloring to a familiar word, in short, to produce a metaphor—is analogous to the flexibility of the vestibular system that allows us to sense imbalance and adjust our muscles and limbs as we walk on even slightly uneven ground.[6]

Spolsky emphasises the unconsciousness of this flexibility, 'it is not something even philosophers pay regular attention to'. Scientific studies certainly frequently describe the balance required during gait, and the rhythms of the gait, as automatic functions, not usually requiring conscious control.[7] Alemán's writing, however, deliberately draws our attention both to the rhythm and style of Guzmán's gait and to the balancing-act of multiple interpretations as he juxtaposes Guzmán's vain interpretation of his strutting and limping body with the contrasting harsher judgements of Guzmán's milieux, and the omniscient view of the Guzmán-narrator which encompasses both. For Spolsky, when surprising meanings threaten to cause the reader to 'swerve', this reader's unconscious self-stabilising abilities enable them to continue moving smoothly through the text without (as Aristotle says), stumbling, hitting their toe, and falling flat. Alemán however often wants us to stumble, to notice when we fall or come to a halt together with Guzmán, and thereby to reflect on walking as a metaphor for moral life.

James Mabbe, translator of Spanish literary and religious works and companion to ambassador John Digby in Spain, translated *Guzmán de Alfarache* into English as *The Rogue* (1622).[8] *The Rogue* was popular, seeping into wider culture; Lena Liapi relates that 'Gusman' became English slang for any seventeenth-century highwayman.[9] Mabbe is attentive to the gait; often adding, in the course of translation, gait-related vocabulary not present in the original Spanish text. Occasionally, he does so as a rhetorical flourish, a calling-card as a translator. For instance, *Deuout Contemplations*, Mabbe's translation of Spanish mystic Cristóbal de Fonseca's *Discursos*, embellishes the walking imagery Fonseca uses to describe a Canaanite woman's request that Christ exorcise her daughter. Fonseca simply describes Christ 'going more' than the woman ('anduvo lo mas ... y ella lo menos'), cueing Mabbe to introduce more explicit vocabulary of stepping and journeying: 'though Christ had the longer and harder Journey of it, and she the shorter and easier; yet you see shee was willing to put the best foot forward, and to take some paines her selfe in the businesse'.[10] Mabbe expands Fonseca's statement that the woman put in some of her own work ('algun trabajo'), adding an image of this work as an earnest, faithful step, 'shee was willing to put the best foot forward'.[11] At other times, as in his translation of Guzmán's church strut, Mabbe Englishes the gait in a manner that skews Alemán's writing.

Mabbe and Alemán share a wider early modern European tendency to scrutinise bodily comportment, including gait, for signs of good or bad breeding. This is partly due to the body of conduct literature circulating in translation and original between Britain and Continental Europe. However, whilst Alemán's concern with behaviour was inflected by Iberian anxieties about distinguishing Old Christians from conversos, Mabbe's translations are shaped by theories about reading an individual's national identity in their gait and behaviour. Mabbe was one of several late-sixteenth and early-seventeenth-century translators who catered to many English readers' fascination with Spain and Catholicism. Translators met their readers' perceived appetite for derogatory, othering depictions of Spain by emphasising the danger and discomfort of Spanish life and highlighting the 'Spanishness' of texts they translated by marking particular episodes and characters as revelatory about Spanish national identity.[12] As Giorgio Riello explains, early modern discussions of walking often xenophobically represented the walker's gait and posture as tied to their ethnicity.[13] If translation is a form of walking together, Mabbe often walks in step with Alemán, and sometimes twists the direction of their journey.

Alemán's Guzmán relates, 'I got myself up all fancy' ('púseme de ostentación') before heading to church. Mabbe makes gait part of Guzmán's gallant wardrobe, something 'put on' along with the fancy clothes, 'I . . . put on a proud and stately gate'. Mabbe compounds the emphasis on walking by adding 'I did strut':

> I got me up betimes one Sunday morning, put on a proud and stately gate; and in all this my gallantrie, stept me with a jolly presence into the Cathedrall church, for to heare Masse, though (let me whisper it in your eare) I went thither more (I feare me) for ostentiation than devotion; not so much to hear, as to be seen. I walkt round the Church some three or four times at least; I visited the Chappels (which were most resorted unto) til at last I came between the two Quires, where I staid: There I saw many Ladies and Gentlewomen and a great many of Gallants. But I did strut and set forth my selfe as I had been the onely Cocke of the game, and all the rest Crauens; none of their combes nor feathers were so goodly (me thought) as mine owne. I did put them downe all for a braue suit of clothes. And like a bonny-Shepheard, made show of all the whole fleece, as one that was very willing, that they

should take a generall suruey both of my person, and Apparell, not debarring their eies of those lesser obiects, as my girdle, garters, and shoo-ties, which were all *del Tudesco*, curious and delicate worke, right *Flanders*.

I stretcht forth my necke, bore out my brest, stood stiffe vpon my legs, aduancing one while this, and then that other foot; carrying my selfe in that vaine and idle fashion, that euery one at last had found me out, and obseruing the strangenesse of my looks my Mimick gestures, and often change of Postures, they began to iest and scoffe at my folly. But as long as they lookt vpon me, I ne're lookt into that; nor did I so much as once perceiue, that my faults were the strings whereon their laughter plaid. But I rather thought with my selfe, that they did admire my curiositie, and my gallantrie.[14]

Following Alemán, Mabbe undercuts Guzmán's self-regard with the humorous simile of the puffed-up cockerel. 'Strut' is always associated with an inflated sense of self-importance, and with a body distended, puffed-out, and stiff.[15] 'Advancing one while this, and then that other foot' is Mabbe's addition to the Spanish (neither is it in Barezzo Barezzi's 1615 Italian translation, which Mabbe also drew on), and seems redundant at first: an unnecessary pedantic description of the basics of walking.[16] However, as this phrase makes us almost tediously conscious of a usually automatic process, it highlights the excessive thought Guzmán puts into his gait. The plethora of words separating the (pro)nouns 'this' and 'foot' which represent Guzmán's planted feet, 'one while . . . and then that other', evoke Guzmán dangling his feet for some time in the air before planting them on the ground. The clause arrangement suggests his second foot lifts after 'this', stretches in mid-air for as long as it takes to say 'and then that other', then makes contact with the church floor in front of him at the word 'foot'. This strengthens Alemán's cockerel image, deliberate stretching and planting of feet being a walking style characteristic of chickens. Guzmán previously established himself as flamboyantly birdlike, describing how he 'peacocked around Toledo' ('di ciertas pavonadas por Toledo').[17]

Mabbe's focus on national identity occludes Alemán's emphasis on Guzmán's difference from his milieu. Fellow translator Leonard Digges' dedicatory poem to *The Rogue* praises Mabbe's 'Margent'; Alemán did not include marginalia in *Guzmán de Alfarache* whereas Mabbe introduces copious marginal notes to explain Spanish puns or key terms and to comment on the narrative, often indicating that the novel reveals the behaviours of *Spanish* people specifically.[18] Mabbe's marginalia render Guzmán less distinguishable from his milieu by reducing Guzmán to a national stereotype; the marginal note to the church strutting scene reads, 'The Spaniard hath naturally a proud kinde of gate'.[19] Alemán's Guzmán is the only strutting cockerel in the church. Mabbe's Guzmán stands out less strikingly because under Mabbe's gaze, the other Spanish worshippers all also become chickens displaying their combs and feathers, 'none of their combes nor feathers were so goodly (me thought) as mine owne'.

Mabbe's crude over-instruction of his reader overlays Alemán's multi-layered representation of Guzmán learning, and resisting learning, from other bodies and texts. I argue that Guzmán's resistance to Christian social norms offers a complex potential for celebration. On the one hand, Guzmán's recalcitrance to learn 'good Christian behaviour' might be said to align with Inquisitorial anxieties about converso assimilation in Old Christian society. Conversos experienced discrimination and persecution based on notions that Jewish heredity persisted in the gestures and inclinations of the converso body; as Ryan Giles describes, the idea was that no amount of Christian cultural shaping could wholly change the person's inherited 'traits and propensities'.[20] Within this context, Guzmán's persistence in following 'bad' models, strutting and feigning lameness, offers a powerful resistance to pressures to conform humbly and contribute productively to Christian society. No matter how much he is mocked and shamed, Guzmán steps forth with resilience, humour, and renewed hope.

Guzmán's Pedagogical Texts: God and the Beggar's Book

In Part 2, Book 3, Alemán reflects on and consolidates the close relationship between walking and (anti-)learning at play throughout the novel when he compares a person learning to be good to a child learning to walk. The good person walks with and towards God like a child walking with their parent's support:

> It seems to us, when we are drowning in needs that he [God] has forgotten us. But he is like the father who, teaching his son to walk, leaves him alone for a little, pretending to have abandoned him. If the child goes towards his father, even if he only moves his feet a little bit, when he falls his father will receive him in outstretched arms, not allowing him to fall to the ground. However if the child sits down as soon as he is left alone, if he doesn't want to walk, if he doesn't move his feet, and if he lets himself fall as soon as he is set loose, it is not the loving father's fault but the fault of the lazy son.

> Parécenos, cuando nos vemos ahogados en la necesidad, que se olvida de nosotros y es como el padre, que, para enseñar a su hijo que ande, hace como que lo suelta de la mano, déjalo un poco, fingiendo apartarse dél. Si el niño va hacia su padre, por poquito que mude los pies, cuando ya se cae, viene a dar en sus brazos y en ellos lo recibe, no dejándolo llegar a el suelo; empero, si apenas lo ha dejado, cuando luego se sienta, si no quiere andar, si no mueve los pies y si en soltándolo se deja caer, no es la culpa del amoroso padre sino del perezoso niño.[21]

Lapsing into shorter asyndetic clauses, Alemán's prose slows and stumbles, mimicking the jerky series of events it describes as the child toddles forward, falls, is scooped into its parent's arms, narrowly misses the floor, sits down, won't walk. The order of events in the final sentence suggests that the child gravitates twice towards the ground, getting up in between: first he sits down and then again 'falls': the lazy child is let go ('lo ha dejado'), then sits down ('se sienta') and doesn't want to walk ('no quiere andar') nor move his feet ('no mueve los pies') and finally allows himself to fall ('se deja caer'). This implies that God gives the naughty child a couple of chances at standing upright and walking before branding him 'lazy' ('perezoso').

Guzmán explicitly casts himself as this naughty child at various points in the novel, both through his calamitous vain walks and indolent refusals to walk, and through moral statements deploying walking imagery; 'I determined to be good', Guzmán reflects of his life straight after the toddler analogy, 'but I tired myself out after a couple of steps' ('Determinábame a ser bueno; cansábame a dos pasos').[22] Attempting to make changes in his life too quickly, he states, 'Hee that walkes too fast, will be quickly weary'.[23] However, Alemán complicates easy analogies between falling and wickedness, and physical and moral 'uprightness'; inclining towards the ground is also a sign of devotion. Guzmán takes his first 'steps' into Rome in 1.3.6 with exaggerated humble piety, using his mouth; 'The first step that I placed inside Rome was with my mouth, kissing that sacred ground' ('El primer paso que dentro puse, fue con la boca, besando aquel santo suelo').[24] Alemán's Guzmán walks *with* his kiss: the mouth functions as a kind of foot, something Mabbe's translation does not capture. Mabbe writes as if the kiss is a completely new activity once walking has stopped, rather than a continuation of it, 'The first step that I set within those holy gates, I fell downe on my face, and kist that hallowed ground'.[25] Walking throughout *Guzmán* is a sign of Guzmán's moral status; though Mabbe lets this particular instance slip through the net, a kiss can be a step because it is imbued with moral significance.

The Bible frequently figures a good life as a walk with God; early moderns frequently explored the kinesic possibilities of this image. Alemán imagines it in kinesic terms of trusting that God will catch us if we slip up as long as we are making an effort and moving in the right direction. The first person to walk with God in the Bible was Enoch, who 'walked with God three hundred years' (Genesis 5.24). English Bibles continue to favour the phrase 'Enoch walked with God' (which appears twice in this passage, before Enoch disappears), including early modern editions such as the King James, Douay-Rheims, and Geneva translations. The 1602 Spanish Reina-Valera edition similarly states that Enoch 'walked' (caminó) with God: 'Y caminó Henoch con Dios'. This translates the Hebrew root *hâlakh*, which can mean continuous locomotion ('going'), as well as a manner of living and behaving. English translators commonly render *hâlakh* literally and figuratively as 'walk'. The Latin states baldly that Enoch 'walked' ('ambulavit'); the Greek Septuagint dispenses with ideas of locomotion altogether, using the verb *euaresteō* (I am well pleasing): 'Enoch was well pleasing to God'. The English 'Enoch walked with God' captures the idea that Enoch's life harmonised with God's will whilst leaving open the possibility that Enoch was having a physical kinaesthetic experience. Early modern writers seized on the latter possibility, examining, for instance, how long we might walk with God before growing tired, whether we should match our strides exactly to God's to show that we are good followers, or whether hanging back and letting God walk ahead would demonstrate this better.[26]

Authors often ran into difficulties with this metaphor: is walking with God, which suggests some commensurability between us and God, even possible given the huge difference between a finite human being and their omnipotent Creator? In *Brotherly Reconcilement* (1605), Church of England clergyman Egeon Askew reads Genesis alongside the *Aeneid* to consider how Christians might pace themselves when following God,

> if we cannot like *Henock* walke with God, nor treade in the steppes of our heauenly Father, (for who can take such a steppe of loue as did God, from heauen his throne to earth his footstoole?) yet as that boy *Ascanius* followed his father, *non passibus aequis*, let vs follow him though with vnequall paces: let vs walke with Christ our elder brother, who in this path went before vs, and *left vs an example that we should follow his steppes*.[27]

Askew's marginal note says 'our elder brother's example': good walking means attempting (even unsuccessfully) to follow a divinely-laid-out path. Askew captures metaphorical meanings—to follow God's steps, for instance, is to follow his precepts—but keeps kinesic understanding in play as we imagine our childlike 'unequall paces' compared to God's space-travelling 'steppe of loue'. When Askew interpolates the image of God using earth as his footstool, a sudden image of God with giant feet destabilises the scenario in which we walk proportionately along with him. The mystery of incarnation is suggested in this step whereby God steps down from heaven to live on earth as a man whilst remaining a giant being who rests his feet on earth. Conflicting kinesic impulses, provoked by simultaneously contemplating the resting foot and the stepping foot, exemplify the difficulty of the metaphor of walking with God and (bringing the readers back to a befitting Christian humility) defy any assumption that we can fully understand or imagine God.

In his rendering of 'walking with God' in the toddler analogy, Alemán is most interested in falling, being upright, making effort, and being close to or far from God. Most important to Alemán is whether the child attempts to walk towards God at all, 'even if he only moves his feet a little bit'. For Mabbe, *how* the child walks – the style of his gait – is equally if not more important.[28] While Alemán's father leaves his child alone, Mabbe's does so specifically 'to see how he will shift his feet'. While Alemán's good child moves his feet 'a little', Mabbe tells us how he moves them 'walking softly, and with trembling steps'. In Mabbe's translation, it is no longer enough for the good child to try and walk, he must walk at the right tempo, and not be too slow nor (as Mabbe repeats twice) 'make too much haste'. For Mabbe, walking with God with an unseemly 'sweate and puffe' is as impious as failing to try and walk with him at all:

> It seemeth vnto vs, that when we are swallowed vp as it were with desperation; and that want and pouerty lye heauy vpon vs, that hee is forgetfull and vnmindfull of vs; when as indeed, he is but like vnto that father, who for to teach his sonne to goe, maketh as if he did loosen his hand from him, faigning to let him goe alone by him-selfe, and for a while to see how hee will shift his feete, stands in some neere distance from him, yet not so farre off, but that hee still keepes him-selfe close by his side, and when walking softly, and with trembling steps towards him, he sees him ready to fall, he runnes in vnto him, and catching him in his armes, receiues him into them, and embraces him, not suffering him to fall to the ground. But when the father hath no sooner left him to him-selfe, but that either he makes too much haste, or will not goe at all, nor so much as offer to moue a foot, or letting goe his hold, vnfastning him-selfe from his fathers hands, he comes to catch a fall, the fault is not in the father, but in the sonnes either too much dulnesse, or too much haste.[29]

Emphasising the style of walking, Mabbe imbues this passage with one of the novel's key concerns: that the style of Guzmán's gait has moral, religious valence.

Alemán brands the child who doesn't walk 'perezoso' (lazy, slow, tired) which Mabbe translates as 'too much dulnesse' suggesting at once physical and mental sluggishness. In Part 1 Book 3, Alemán describes how Guzmán learns to be 'perezoso' through mimicking a beggar and his book, exploring the moral connotations of his leg's 'dulnesse'. The beggar gives Guzmán a copy of the beggars' law (*Ordenanzas Mendicativas*) which delimits behaviour, possessions, and appearance for a beggar, including their walk ('it shall be only lawfull for them', Mabbe translates, 'to walke with two Crutches and a fore legge, with a long and deepe tent in it').[30] Drawing on this book and his own experience, the beggar teaches Guzmán to modify his voice, clothing, body, and behaviour in order to appear sick and disabled, thus attracting the maximum charitable donations. Guzmán describes it as an 'art' ('arte') to pretend to be leprous, with a swollen leg, artificial ulcers, made-up face, and motionless arm:

> he taught me to fake leprosy, create ulcers, puff up a leg, lose movement in an arm, tint my face's hue, alter my whole body, and other curious principles of the art.
>
> [E]nseñome a fingir lepra, hacer llagas, hinchar una pierna, tullir un brazo, teñir el color del rostro, alterar todo el cuerpo y otros primores curiosos del arte.[31]

The church strut established Guzmán's stiff legs as morally suspect; the toddler analogy links lazy legs with moral laziness. In between these two, the episode with the beggar explores the failure to move one's feet and arms (which Alemán expresses through synonyms 'entullecer' and 'tullir': to lose activity [in a limb]) as a metaphor for moral and social apathy. Guzmán reflects of his career as a beggar,

> Once men open their mouths to beg, closing their eyes to shame, and tie their hands up rather than work, losing the activity of ['entulleciendo'] their feet at will, their badness has no remedy.
>
> Después que una vez los hombres abren las bocas al pedir, cerrando los ojos à la vergüenza, y atan las manos para el trabajo, entulleciendo los pies a la solicitud, no tiene su mal remedio.[32]

Sitting on the ground to beg rather than walking and working, Guzmán is the naughty child with his soul in peril.

Applying his newly-acquired 'art', Guzmán focuses on his leg. In the church strut Guzmán drew attention to and with his stiffened legs; when begging he uses a slowed, puffed, painted leg to draw onlookers' gazes. Guzmán deploys a herbal concoction to falsely makes his leg seem 'incurably cancerous' for a short time.[33] Entering a church to beg rather than strut, Guzmán bears traces of his church strut in his body as he 'began to stretch [his] throate' and 'drest [him] such a legge, that was very well worth more than a very good vine-yard' (i.e., generated more profit than a fertile vineyard).[34] The beggar's rulebook and coaching give Guzmán a script and direction for his performance, but eventually he incorporates this learning so thoroughly into his body that he has no more need of them: 'lifting up the cloth with a tender finger to shew unto them, what a grievous sore legge I had, wherein I was so ready, and so perfect, that I had need to no body to teach me my lesson'.[35] As Katherine Schaap Williams, Lindsey Row-Heyveld and Lauren Coker explain, early modern texts represent feigned disability in explicitly theatrical terms; even real disabilities were theatrically displayed for appraisal and charity, with 'cures' staged and scripted.[36] Row-Heyveld emphasises the prominence of false disability and associated fake miracle-cures in English rogue literature.[37] The miracle-cure script is also the theme of Chapter 4 of this book, which deals with a diabolical 'cure' for aphasia. By the time he meets the beggar, Guzmán is a more seasoned, cunning rogue than when he struts through church, enabling him to take control of the script. As a result, he is slightly more successful at manipulating others' appraisals of him and more able to turn the situation to his own advantage when his deception is uncovered.

As with the church strut, when Guzmán sits to beg his leg is a textual and bodily discrepancy that wobbles Alemán's prose. Festering and seemingly-immobile, the leg looks disproportionately bad compared to the rude health of the rest of Guzmán's body. Alemán's prose emphasises this, like several early modern authors linking physical disability and uneven prosody, letting the leg hang out of the end of the first sentence spoken below by the town governor who has come to scrutinise Guzmán.[38] Guzmán recounts that the governor asks,

> "With those colours and freshness of body, given that you are fat, blooming, and firm, how is it that you have a leg like this? The one does not really agree with the other". I responded, perturbed, "I don't know sir, God has been served by it."

> Con esos colores y frescura de cuerpo, que estás gordo, recio y tieso, ¿cómo tienes así esa pierna? No acuden bien lo uno a lo otro. Respondíle turbado: No sé señor, Dios ha sido servido dello.[39]

The governor establishes Guzmán's healthily coloured, fresh body – his generally fat, blooming, and firm figure – before travelling with his eyes and prose to the odd leg.

The governor's question suggests confusion; Guzmán himself is likewise 'perturbed' ('turbado'), suppositive of a disruption of bodily and textual order. 'Turbado' can mean confused, interrupted when speaking, and prevented from following a natural course of events. Mabbe's translation emphasises rupture in speech, 'I answered him, but with a troubled kinde of deliuery'.[40] When the governor sends for a surgeon to solve the mystery, the surgeon seems to catch Guzmán's perturbed state: the anomaly of Guzmán's body initially 'perturbed him' ('turbelo'). It is an example of what Schaap Williams identifies as the 'unfixable form' of disability; cultural constructions of the early modern disabled body as blurred and hard to categorise.[41] The governor's questioning leaves Guzmán doubting his expertise as a trickster, the surgeon questioning his own medical expertise. Finally, the surgeon fixes Guzmán, labelling the leg healthy and using his own healthy eyes as a standard of measurement:

He sent for a surgeon, that he might examine me. He came and looked at me for a while. To begin with, it perturbed him that he didn't know what was going on; later he was undeceived and he said "Sir this young man does not have anything more wrong with his leg than I do with my eyes."

Mandó llamar un cirujano que me examinase. Vino y miróme de espacio. A los principios turbélo, que no sabía qué fuse; más luego se desengaño y le dijo, Señor, este mozo no tiene más en su pierna que yo en los ojos.[42]

The surgeon experiences what Spolsky calls a 'swerve': an anomaly in the usual smooth march of events, fittingly exemplified in a leg that does *not* march smoothly. With his final diagnosis, the surgeon overcomes this issue that had threatened to trip him up: 'this young man does not have anything more wrong with his leg than I do with my eyes'.

There ensues a fight for control of this already unsteady miniature performance, and of the narrative. In a theatrical revelation, the surgeon removes Guzmán's leg-coverings, to reveal 'a perfectly healthy leg'. According to Guzmán, the spectator at this show wondered ('quedó ... admirado') at the sight, 'the governor was lost in admiration at seeing me in this manner, and most of all he admired my skill' ('Quedó el gobernador admirado en verme de aquella manera, y más de mi habilidad').[43] Like early modern English 'admire', Spanish 'admirar' can mean 'to wonder at' or 'be impressed by' something but also just to look at something because it is surprising or extraordinary.[44] Both words derive from Latin 'admirari' (to respect or wonder at, but also to be surprised or astonished by). The sense is not necessarily positive: the governor may be 'admiring' Guzmán's leg simply because it seems particularly weird, roguish, or shocking. One wonders whether to wholly believe Guzmán's statement that the governor was positively admiring his skill ('habilidad'). Mabbe had available to him pervasive English anxieties about bodies disabled through English-Spanish military conflict and concomitant xenophobic associations of disabled Spanish bodies and sexual and violent degeneracy. However, his translation dwells only on the surgeon and governors' exploration of Guzmán's body, and the xenophobic asides populating his margin fall silent, 'that which did astonish him most, was how I should haue the aptitude and wit to doe such a thing as this'.[45]

The governor, suspecting Guzmán was a fraud all along, aimed to teach him a lesson by calling the surgeon. However, Guzmán stoutly refuses to change his behaviour; he simply moves town and continues the same trick, amplifying his roguery by rising (or falling) to the status of a false Christ. In the next town he begs in, Guzmán's seemingly debilitating leg cancer touches the heart of a Cardinal, who calls for surgeons to treat Guzmán. Guzmán hears the surgeons preparing to cut, cauterise, and perhaps amputate his leg, and then (having discovered Guzmán's deception) plotting to apply an expensive, painful, unnecessary cure to wring money from the Cardinal. Realising that they are crooks like him, Guzmán strikes a deal with the surgeons, promising to help them dupe the Cardinal. Guzmán seems to glory in his ascendancy over the Cardinal who is merely following Christ's injunction to care for the poor as in so doing one cares for God (Matthew 10:42). Guzmán is delighted to occupy the role of deity, revelling in the fact that the Cardinal 'did not see me as a man: I seemed to him God himself'.[46] As Andrew Gordon explains, early modern worshippers venerated Christ's bloody footprints, suggesting they held Christ's pained gait carefully in their minds.[47] It is not Guzmán's limp that makes him wicked, but the fact that his gait is deceitfully contrived – a false emulation of Christ's disabled body.

When Guzmán visits Zaragoza in 2.3.1, he confronts the novel's pervasive interrelation between walking body and text as each sculpts the other. In Zaragoza, he reads the 'Arancel de Necedades': a list of ludicrous rules for behaviour with incommensurate and seemingly random punishments that satirises contemporary conduct literature such as Giovanni Della Casa's *Il Galateo* (1558). The Arancel condemns several 'foolish crimes' related to gait; the first rule states, 'To those who walk around the street talking to themselves when they are alone, or who do so at home: We condemn them as fools for three months'.[48] The second rule stipulates the same punishment for people who decide where to place their feet based on the arrangement of cracks or ['and' in some early editions] stones in the pavement.[49] People who touch the walls as they walk are afforded six months' approbation. The Arancel moves on to condemn such heinous sins as 'painting on the walls or sketching on the ground' with one's urine (a form of disorderly writing?) and frequently asking 'are we nearly there?' whilst on journeys.[50] Guzmán risks making a hefty donation to a hospital because he blows his nose into a handkerchief; his host in Zaragoza rushes to show him the final stipulation in the 'Arancel de Necedades', lifted from Della Casa: not to blow one's nose and gaze into the handkerchief 'as if it contained pearls'.[51] The Arancel forces Guzmán to confront the ways in which his gait has been shaped by, and retains the capacity to resist, social norms. Guzmán laughs at this document; his laugh recognises the ludic, comic potential of breaking social norms that he so often exploits himself, and challenges the authority of such codes of conduct.

Conclusion: Against Learning – Guzmán and the Widow

Guzmán consolidates his roguish cunning through mimicry, resisting the lessons that keepers of social norms wish to teach him, and learning better to survive in (what he believes is) a generally false, cutthroat society. Thereby, Alemán explores kinesic and kinaesthetic experience as sites simultaneously of learning and failure to learn. Sustained across a sizeable two-part novel, Guzmán's resistance to learning is impressive. Though he is beaten up, tricked, nearly unnecessarily operated on, and generally berated both by others and by himself for his stiff, stretching, overly conscious, vainglorious gait, he persists with it. It is hard not to be struck by, hard not to be tempted to celebrate, the strength of Guzmán's individuality, tested repeatedly against the weight of Christian societal machinery.

Guzmán exemplifies this in 2.3.2 when, long after the feigned disability, he displays the same style of gait he was maligned for in church when he struts past the balcony of a rich widow he has designs on. He displays a modicum of self-awareness and learning, but an overall resistance to change. Alemán's description of Guzmán's puffed-out belly and stiffened legs at this point is strikingly similar to the church strut; both involve the verb *atiesar* (to stiffen) and depict Guzmán inviting and misreading others' gazes. When the widow turns with her servants to watch him and they all smile down at him, Guzmán vaingloriously believes he is in luck,

> With this, it already seemed to me that my job was done. With stiffened legs and chest and lifted neck, I passed by her twice or thrice, the edge of my cloak over my shoulder, my hat placed in the air and my eyes darting around to watch every step such that they grinned not a little and I was satisfied.

> Ya con esto me pareció hecho mi negocio. Atiesé de piernas y pecho y, levantado el pescuezo, dile dos o tres paseos, el canto de capote por cima del hombro, el sombrero puesto en el aire y levando tornátiles los ojos, volviendo a mirar a cada paso, de que no poco estaban risueñas y yo satisfecho.[52]

Mabbe similarly echoes his own earlier rendering of the church strut, reusing verbs of stretching and stiffness. In church, Mabbe's Guzmán states, 'I stretcht forth my necke, bore out my brest, stood stiffe vpon my legs'; before the widow, he relates, 'I stretcht out my legs, and my brest, and lifting vp my head, and bearing vp my necke somewhat stiffe'. While in the church strut he 'advance[d] one while this, and then that other foot', before the widow, Guzmán 'tread[ed] [his] steps in state'. Mabbe's Guzmán explains, having 'spent that day in walking up and downe',

I stretcht out my legs, and my brest, and lifting vp my head, and bearing vp my necke somewhat stiffe, I made two or three short turnes, throwing one corner of my cloake ouer my shoulder, setting my hat on t'one side, laying my left hand on my sword, and resting the right on my side, treading my steps in state, and turning my rolling eyes vpon her, I walk't leysurely before her window, my eye being neuer off on her. Whereat they laugh't a good; and I rested well contented. They made themselues merry, and I was very well pleased.[53]

Characteristically, Mabbe adds emphasis on locomotion to the Spanish original by inserting the phrases 'treading my steps in state', 'I walk't leysurely'. By stereotyping Guzmán's nationality, Mabbe's marginal note beside the episode with the widow resonates with his marginalia beside the church strut: 'the Spanish posture: when they court their Mistresse'. Mabbe's parallelism and repetition of sense in the final two sentences in the long quotation above suggest a link between the women's laughter and Guzmán's own contentment. This highlights a new possibility: was Guzmán was deliberately trying to make the women laugh, mimicking his earlier strutting self for the fun of it?

In the episode with the widow, Guzmán's gait prompts self-reflection of a generally egotistical kind. Echoing his description of himself in Book 1 as the prize cockerel, Guzmán compares himself to other gallants, letting his eyes linger depreciatively on their legs and feet: one is handsome except for his feet, Guzmán muses, another but for his legs; he (Guzmán) is the only completely perfect man, 'todo perfecto'.[54] He feels ready to make his move on the widow, 'my job was done' he affirms as he struts beneath her window. When he returns home, Guzmán becomes pensive. Displaying more capacity for self-reflection and a more swiftly-dawning awareness of his milieu's potential mixed attitudes towards him than he did in Book 1, Guzmán thinks through the potential consequences of his strut. He speculates that the widow may be planning a trick on him so, rather than allowing his legs to get him into trouble again, he decides to leave the city right away.[55] There is a kind of kinaesthetic learning at play: replicating the stiff, puffed-out posture of his ill-fated church strut activates Guzmán's memories, stored in his body, of the past consequences of this vainglorious behaviour. Nevertheless, given Guzmán's repeated return to immoral walking up to this point, it is hard to believe that he has now learned a humble lesson once and for all.

Despite the often dubious moral awakenings peppering the novel ('I was too gullible', Guzmán muses after the church; 'I cheated God and the deserving poor', he acknowledges after meeting the Cardinal), Guzmán's legs tell a different story. Critics have often debated whether

Alemán intends *Guzmán* didactically to condemn irreligious ways or whether it is in fact a celebration Guzmán's incorrigible roguishness.[56] As we have seen, Guzmán's gait embodies this ambiguity. There is power in choosing to appreciate Guzmán's strut as a flamboyant, joyous celebration of his body, and in responding to it (as, on one reading, the widow and her women do) with hearty joy and mirthful release rather than moral condemnation. His body's resistance to social norms imposed through humiliation, violence, and legal punishments suggests a strength of embodied individuality that we might find particularly appealing, particularly when we consider Guzmán (as he has been considered) as a queer converso asserting himself in a world that privileged heteronormative, Old Christian values. Juan Diego Vila suggests that each time Guzmán is knocked down for transgressing norms, and each time he reinvents himself, he displays 'the ability to dream and to think of oneself renewed every day, free of the painful subjection of minorities through insults and discrimination'.[57] For Carlos Antonio Rodríguez Matos, Guzmán's queer, 'effeminate' features are the best proof that he is his father's son.[58] Vila suggests that Guzmán owns his (queer, converso) heritage by adopting a stance of pride towards whatever other people try and shame him about, 'in his suffering, Guzmán understands that the only way out is to make "a name from a bad name"; in adversity, he discovers that the only force that one can use to confront the feeling of shame is, in effect, pride'.[59] As we have seen, Guzmán's body comes to the fore in *Guzmán de Alfarache*, its weight and vigour denting the text and buckling Alemán's clauses. Ultimately, I argue, no matter what ostensible morals the narrative draws about Guzmán's un-Christian behaviour, the most impressive image the novel leaves us with is that of Guzmán's incorrigible body. A man wiggling his way through a grand church is in itself a striking image; the impression gains power if we read this man as a queer converso dancing in the seat of the domineering religion that oppressed his family.

Both this chapter and the introduction to this book problematised the idea that kinesic mimicking offers a desirable form of learning. In the introduction, Thomas Ellwood and his father Walter mimicked each other's gait and speed of locomotion: Thomas mimics Walter in order to escape him; Walter mimics Thomas in order to catch and presumably assault him. The next chapter examines the ways in which sectarian religion manifests in Thomas Ellwood's resistant body. Thomas's unbending legs and waist signalled his Quaker identity and (like Guzmán's legs) were read by others as warranting violent reprisals for its nonconformity. Ellwood's autobiography takes up the question of learning and creating patterns through both body and rhythmic prose I have identified in Alemán's writing, making non-conformist movements part of a deliberately-created pattern that helps to shape a non-conformist self.

Notes

1. Mateo Alemán, *Guzmán de Alfarache* ed. Francisco Rico (Madrid: Planeta, 1983), 322. All English translations from Spanish, unless attributed to James Mabbe, are my own.
2. See Bolens, *The Style of Gestures*, 40.
3. See Janel Mueller, 'Periodos', in Sylvia Adamson, Gavin Alexander, and Katrin Ettenhuber, eds *Renaissance Figures of Speech* (Cambridge: Cambridge University Press, 2007) (61–77), 62–3 for discussion of Aristotle's *Rhetoric* and passim for wider discussion of the walking trope in classical rhetorical manuals; for early modern examples see Robert Stagg, 'Staging the Road: Walking, Talking, Footing', in Lisa Hopkins and Bill Angus, eds, *Reading the Road: From Shakespeare's Crossways to Bunyan's Highways* (Edinburgh: Edinburgh University Press, 2020) (185–201), 189–90.
4. Aristotle, *The Art of Rhetoric*, trans. J. H. Freese (Cambridge, Massachusetts: Loeb Classical Library, 1926), 388–9.
5. Ellen Spolsky, *The Contracts of Fiction: Cognition, Culture, Community* (Oxford: Oxford University Press, 2015), 23.
6. Spolsky, *The Contracts of Fiction*, 23–4.
7. Volker Dietz, 'Organization of Human Locomotion: Proprioception and Quadrupedal Coordination', in George Koob et al., eds, *Encyclopedia of Behavioural Neuroscience* (Elsevier, 2010), 490–6. Cf Marie-Pascale Côté, Lynda Murray, and Maria Knikou, 'Spinal Control of Locomotion: Individual Neurons, Their Circuits and Functions', *Frontiers in Physiology* 9 (2018), Article 784, 1–27.
8. David Kathman, 'Mabbe [Mab], James' (2004), https://doi.org/10.1093/ref:odnb/17319 [accessed 23/06/2019]. For cross-pollination between Mabbe's various Spanish-English translations, see John Yamamoto-Wilson, 'James Mabbe's Achievement in His Translation of *Guzmán de Alfarache*', *Translation and Literature*, 8(2) (1999), 137–56.
9. Lena Liapi, *Roguery in Print: Crime and Culture in Early Modern London* (Suffolk: Boydell, 2019), 150–1.
10. 'Don Diego Puede-Ser' [i.e. James Mabbe], *Deuout Contemplations* (London: Adam Islip: 1629), N1v-N2r. The pseudonym is a translational pun; 'puede ser' means 'maybe' ('Mabbe').
11. Cristóbal de Fonseca, *Discursos Para Todos Los Evangelios de la Quaresma* (Madrid: Alonso Martin de Balboa, 1614), O2v.
12. For discussion, see P. E. Russell, 'A Stuart Hispanist: James Mabbe', *Bulletin of Hispanic Studies* 30(118) (1953) (75–85), 84; Paul Salzman, 'Travelling or Staying In: Spain and the Picaresque in the Early 1620s', *The Yearbook of English Studies*, 41(1) (2011), (141–55), 141; John Yamamoto-Wilson, 'Mabbe's Maybes: A Stuart Hispanist in Context', *Translation*

      and Literature 21(3) (2012), 319–42; Anne Cruz, 'Sonnes of the Rogue: Picaresque Relations in England and Spain', in Giancarlo Maiorino, ed., *The Picaresque* (Minnesota University Press, 1996) (248–72), 250.
13. Giorgio Riello, 'The Material Culture of Walking: Spaces of Methodologies in the Long Eighteenth Century', in Catherine Richardson and Tara Hamling, eds, *Everyday Objects* (Aldershot: Ashgate, 2010) (41–56), 48.
14. James Mabbe, trans., *The Rogue: or The life of Guzman de Alfarache* (London: [Eliot's Court Press and George Eld] for Edward Blount, 1623[2?]), P2r.
15. OED 'strut', *n*3a, *v*1. An earlier meaning (*n*1b) is 'flaunt in fine attire': an early link with clothing.
16. Barezzo Barezzi, *Vita Del Picaro Guzmano d'Alfarace* (Venice: Barezzo Barezzi, 1606), S2r.
17. Alemán, *Guzmán de Alfarache*, 321. 'Pavonear' ('to show off one's appearance' – derives from 'pavón' – peacock). Real Academia Española, 'pavonear *v*', 'pavón' *n*, dle.rae.es [accessed August 31st 2019].
18. Digges insists that Mabbe improved on Alemán's original, 'So crabbed Canting was his Authors Pen| And phrase, eu'n darke to his owne Country-men;| Till, thankes and praise to this Translators paine,| His Margent, now makes him speake English plaine', Leonard Digges, 'To *Don Diego Puede-Ser* and his Translation of GUZMAN', in Mabbe, *The Rogue*, A4v.
19. Mabbe, *The Rogue*, P2v.
20. On the interrelation of picaresque and converso heredity in *Guzmán*, see Ryan Giles, 'Picaresque Fatherhood: Racial and Literary Heritage in *Guzmán de Alfarache* 1.1', *Neohelicon* 40 (2013), 227–44.
21. Alemán, *Guzmán de Alfarache*, 797.
22. Alemán, *Guzmán de Alfarache*, 798.
23. Mabbe, *The Rogue*, V6r.
24. Alemán, *Guzmán de Alfarache*, 398.
25. Mabbe, *The Rogue*, V2r.
26. For discussion see Matthew Henry's Bible commentary initially published 1708–10 *Exposition of the Old and New Testaments* (Philadelphia: Towar & Hogan, 1828), Genesis 5.
27. Egeon Askew, *Brotherly Reconcilement* (London: [R Field], 1605), I3r.
28. For a discussion of other English writers with this preoccupation, see Andrew Gordon, '*Eastward Ho* and the Traffic of the Stage', in Jowitt and McInnis, *Travel and Drama in Early Modern England: The Journeying Play* (Cambridge: Cambridge University Press, 2018) (92–110), 97–9.
29. Mabbe, *The Rogue*, Zz2r.
30. Alemán, *Guzmán de Alfarache*, 366–70; Mabbe, *The Rogue*, S2r.
31. Alemán, *Guzmán de Alfarache*, 375.
32. Alemán, *Guzmán de Alfarache*, 593.
33. Alemán, *Guzmán de Alfarache*, 399.
34. Mabbe, *The Rogue*, T5v-T6r.
35. Mabbe, *The Rogue*, T6r.
36. Lindsey Row-Heyveld, *Dissembling Disability in Early Modern English Drama* (New York: Palgrave, 2018), 11, 13, 41; Katherine Schaap Williams, 'Strange Virtue: Staging Acts of Cure', in Sujata Iyengar, ed., *Disability, Health, and Happiness in the Shakespearean Body* (London: Routledge,

2014) (93–108), 104; and Lauren Coker, '"There is no suff'ring due":
Metatheatricality and Disability Drag in *Volpone*', in Allison Hobgood and
David Wood, *Recovering Disability in Early Modern England* (Michigan:
Ohio State University Press, 2013) (123–135), 123. On charity and
encouraging visible disability in Catholic Spain, see Teresa Huguet-Termes,
'Madrid Hospitals and Welfare in the Context of the Hapsburg Empire',
Medical History Supplement, 9 (2009) 64–85.
37. Row-Heyveld, *Dissembling Disability*, 11.
38. On metrical mimicry of physical disability, see Susan Anderson, 'Limping and Lameness on the Early Modern Stage' in Leslie C. Dunn, *Performing Disability in Early Modern English Drama* (New York: Palgrave, 2020), 185–207; Robert Stagg, 'Shakespeare's Bewitching Line', *Shakespeare Survey* 71 (2018), 232–41. On early modern editors' use of 'the language of bodily distortion' and cure to describe textual distortion, see Genevieve Love, *Early Modern Theatre and the Figure of Disability* (London: Arden, 2020), 108.
39. Alemán, *Guzmán de Alfarache*, 393.
40. Mabbe, *The Rogue*, T6r.
41. See Katherine Schaap Williams, *Unfixable Forms: Disability, Performance, and Early Modern English Theater* (Ithaca: Cornell University Press, 2021).
42. Alemán, *Guzmán de Alfarache*, 393.
43. Alemán, *Guzmán de Alfarache*, 393.
44. Real Academia Española, 'admirar' https://dle.rae.es/srv/search?m=30&w=admirar [accessed 23.08.2019].
45. Mabbe, *The Rogue*, T6r. On how 'Spanish degeneracy was linked to disability' in early-seventeenth-century English texts, see Joyce Boro, '"Lame Humor" in Beaumont and Fletcher's *Love's Pilgrimage*', in *Performing Disability* (209–32), 210–211.
46. Alemán, *Guzmán de Alfarache*, 398.
47. Andrew Gordon, 'The Renaissance Footprint: The Material Trace in Print Culture from Dürer to Spenser', *Renaissance Quarterly* 71 (2018), 478–529.
48. 'Primeramente, a los que fueren andando, y hablando por la calle consigo mismos, ya solas, o en su casa lo hicieren: Los condenamos a tres meses de necios', Alemán, *Guzmán de Alfarache*, 743. In early editions, ¶ symbols make each 'foolishness' stand out.
49. 'Les que paseándose por alguna pieza ladrillada, o losas de la calle, fueren asentando los pies por las hiladas o[/y] ladrillos, y por el orden dellos, que, si con cuidado hicieren; los condenamos en la misma pena', Alemán, *Guzmán de Alfarache*, 744.
50. Alemán, *Guzmán de Alfarache*, 744–5.
51. Alemán, *Guzmán de Alfarache*, 748.
52. Alemán, *Guzmán de Alfarache*, 754.
53. Mabbe, *The Rogue*, Tt4v.
54. Alemán, *Guzmán de Alfarache*, 754–5.
55. Alemán, *Guzmán de Alfarache*, 756.
56. On the novel as 'didactic', see Paul Salzman, 'Travelling or Staying In: Spain and the Picaresque in the Early 1620s', *The Yearbook of English Studies*, 41(1) (2011) (141–155), 152; Carlos Antonio Rodríguez Matos, *El*

Narrador Pícaro: Guzmán de Alfarache (Madison: The Hispanic Seminary of Medieval Studies, 1985), 1.
57. '[L]a capacidad de soñar y de pensarse nuevo cada día, libre de la dolosa sujeción minoritaría por el insulto y la discriminación', Juan Diego Vila, 'Empero Mi Alma Triste Siempre Padeció Tinieblas: Guzmanillo y el dolor de la sujeción minoritaria', in Michèle Guillemont and Juan Diego Vila, eds, *Para Leer el Guzmán de Alfarache y Otros Textos de Mateo Alemán* (Buenos Aires: Universidad de Buenos Aires, 2015), 223–249, 249.
58. Matos, *El Narrador Pícaro*, 106.
59. 'Guzmán comprende, en su sufrimiento, que la única salida es hacer "nombre de mal nombre"; descubre, en la adversidad, que la única fuerza oponible al sentimiento de vergüenza es, efectivamente, el orgullo', 'Empero Mi Alma Triste Siempre Padeció Tinieblas', 246.

Chapter 3

Plain Plasticity: Thomas Ellwood's *The History of the Life of Thomas Ellwood* (1714)

It is 1659 and Thomas Ellwood has stolen out of the family home to attend a Quaker meeting in secret, spending the night with the Quaker John Rance and his wife. Finding Thomas's bedroom empty, as Thomas relates in his autobiographical *The History of the Life of Thomas Ellwood* (1714), his violently anti-Quaker father Walter falls into 'a Passion of Grief', weeping and fearing that Thomas has been harmed.[1] The following day, Rance calls at the Ellwood household in Oxfordshire to distract Walter, so that Thomas can slip in at the back door. Walter is annoyed to see Rance, a Quaker, in his home, and to learn that Rance knows Thomas. Just as Walter is showing Rance out, Thomas creeps in and runs straight into Walter. Like any good Quaker, Thomas believes all humans are equal and refuses to doff his hat to anyone, including Walter. A respectable mid-seventeenth-century non-Quaker father, Walter expects his son to doff his cap to him. Thomas writes,

> The Sight of my Hat upon my Head made him presently forget that I was that Son of his, whom he had so lately lamented as lost; and his Passion of Grief turning into Anger, he could not contain himself; but running upon me, with both his Hands, first violently snatcht off my Hat, and threw it away; then giving me some Buffets on my Head, he said, *Sirrah, get you up to your Chamber.*
>
> I forthwith went; he following me at the Heels, and now and then giving me a Whirret on the Ear; which (the way to my Chamber lying through the Hall where *John Rance* was) he, poor Man, might see and be sorry for (as I doubt not but he was) but could not help me.[2]

Born in 1639, Thomas is here around 20 years old: between man and boy in Walter's eyes. Walter sends Thomas to his room; excruciatingly, this occurs in front of Rance.

Thomas's description of his walk of shame past Rance seems to elongate out of Thomas's control. The parentheses fail to contain Thomas's words as distinct grammatical units, suggesting that the walk through the hall under Rance's gaze felt embarrassingly drawn out. Though Thomas clips Rance into parentheses, the subsequent reference to Rance, 'he, poor Man', escapes and exceeds this punctuation. These muddled textual boundaries accompany Walter and Thomas's violently-broken interpersonal boundary, in a scene where everyone seems to be in the wrong place at the wrong time. Thomas's cool sympathy for Rance ('poor man') and lack of detail about his own emotions contrast sharply with his emphasis on Walter's tantrum. Walter 'could not contain himself', 'snatcht' Thomas's hat, and, almost stepping on Thomas's 'heels', buffeted and whirreted (sharply hit) him all the way to his room. Thomas implicitly reverses Walter's conception of Thomas as a naughty child in need of discipline: it is Walter who is unable to control his emotions as he switches between extremes of lamentation and rage. Ultimately, rather than an unwelcome onlooker, Rance is Thomas's ally: a fellow Quaker, another victim of Walter.

This chapter examines how *The History* documents and complicates Thomas's resistance to key mainstream social and religious behavioural norms as he adheres instead to a Quaker way of life. Quakers favoured a plain prose style, equating this with honesty; writing simple unadorned prose was in itself one type of Quaker behaviour. Thomas shapes *The History* to accord with the Quaker worldview, casting Walter as the unruly antagonist to Thomas's exemplary Quakerism. However, as we saw in the case of Guzmán in the previous chapter, as Thomas reflects on his life, he seems seduced by his own youthful vigour, troubling his text's even tone. *The History* describes Thomas's path from schoolboy often whipped for pranks and Quaker imprisoned for his faith in Newgate, Bridewell, Aylesbury Gaol, and various correction houses in the early 1660s, to Quaker poet, pamphleteer, and editor living independently of Walter and working as the poet John Milton's amanuensis. Much of the book dwells on Thomas's fraught and increasingly tenuous relationship with Walter, Walter's violence and injustice towards Thomas, and Thomas's friendship with the Quaker Penington family, especially spouses Isaac and Mary Penington and Mary's daughter Giuli.[3] Walter was a local magistrate and Justice of the Peace; his occasional curiosity about religious non-conformity did not extend to accepting Thomas's Quaker faith. We met Thomas in the Introduction when he'd purloined the house keys and slipped out the back door to attend yet another Quaker meeting, Walter giving chase. Moments like this chase and the encounter with Walter and Rance in the hallway originally unfolded quickly and instinctively. However, Thomas writes them as if they are occurring in slow motion, dwelling on the kinesic and kinaesthetic melodies (or, more often, discords) involved, and thereby minutely constructing his masculine Quaker self in tandem with and opposition to other people.

Attending to their Inward Light, Quakers resisted the behavioural codes that mainstream Anglican society attempted to impose on them in order to reinforce social hierarchies.[4] Quakers distinguished themselves by adhering to non-conformist patterns of behaviour; these included a range of behaviours like refusing to kneel in church and to swear oaths, refusing to bow and doff their caps, and using informal 'thou' rather than respectful 'you' with social superiors (including their fathers).[5] Many Quakers rejected Anglican prohibitions against working or riding on the Christian Sabbath. Following the mid-to-late-seventeenth-century founder of Quakerism George Fox's statement that it is better truly to live in God's grace than to say an empty grace with one's lips, Quakers frequently refused to say grace at mealtimes.[6] Their opponents drew on the equations of not saying grace with lust and greed that we saw in Rush's grace in Chapter 1 to attack this; 'R. H.' (potentially the poet Samuel Austin) writes in *The Character of a Quaker* (1671) that 'he cannot endure *Ceremonies* or *Complements*, especially where his Belly is concerned, and therefore falls to all meat (as *Gallants* do to a *Wench* or *Oysters*) *without saying Grace*'.[7] Protestants like Quakers who dissented from the Church of England's practices were known as 'non-conformists'. From the Latin *conformare* (to mould into the same shape), 'non-conformism' was, etymologically, a refusal to let religious, legal, and familial authorities mould one's body and mind into the same shape as other people's. When Quakers resisted it in their families and wider society, the state's shaping hand became a violent hand, whirreting the 'misbehaving' child or wielding a whip at the imprisoned Quaker. Quakers like Thomas resisted conformity through self-shaping in their actions and their writing: building up careful habits of non-conformity to strengthen themselves in Quaker patterns of life.

Aristotle's discussion of habit underlies much early modern and modern thought on the ways in which a person can be moulded through their habitual behaviour. In Book 2 of *Nichomachean Ethics* (c. 340 BCE), Aristotle states that we can acquire a range of qualities through habitual action. A builder becomes a builder through building, a moderate person becomes moderate through practising moderation, and we can become courageous by doing courageous things.[8] As Ramie Targoff has argued, sixteenth- and seventeenth-century religious and political authorities applied this principle to their own ends: producing widespread conformity and obedience to Anglican ideals by demanding that citizens habitually practise submissive gestures like kneeling in church.[9] Quakers created their own non-conformist habits, against the grain of mainstream Anglican society. Thomas tests himself against conformist society, building up Quaker habits until they are his (second) nature. For example, he begins relatively safely by saying 'thou' to old friends and refusing to reciprocate these friends' bows and doffed caps.[10] However on the same day he hides down a back alley to avoid greeting a pair of Justices who know Walter: Thomas does not yet feel ready to address these older, upper class men as 'thou' but does not want to betray his Quaker conscience by calling them 'you'.[11] It is some time, too, before he stops calling Walter 'sir' and 'you'. Eventually, through persistent practice, Thomas is strong enough to own his Quaker faith in front of both legal officials and Walter. Owning his Quakerism with increasing fortitude in the face of violence, imprisonment, and social stigma, Thomas becomes a courageous non-conformist by habitually behaving in a courageous non-conformist way.

The work of the philosopher Catherine Malabou in the first two decades of the twenty-first century illuminates how Thomas seized on his body's malleability (which religious and political authorities wanted to manipulate to shape him into a conforming Anglican subject) and decisively used it to shape *himself*. Drawing on Aristotelian theories of habit and on cognitive neuroscience, Malabou describes the human self as 'plastic': able to shape itself and hold its form, and thereby able to resist the forms that others impose on it.[12] Malabou explains, 'for Aristotle, habit implies the aptitude for change, along with the possibility of preserving the modifications inherent in such a change': the 'twin energies' of 'constancy and creation'.[13] Malabou depicts the plastic human subject negotiating a way between two extremes of plasticity: firstly our fluidity, which enables us to (re)form ourselves; secondly, a certain rigidity which enables us to retain our new identity as our habits solidify into an increasingly intractable second nature.

Malabou posits two options: either we allow society to manipulate our plasticity and shape us to its own ideological ends, or we seize control of our own plasticity and shape ourselves, resisting the attempts of authorities to transform us.[14] For Malabou, the latter option is obviously more desirable. She stresses plasticity's anarchic properties with her idea of 'destructive plasticity', whereby:

> plasticity is also the capacity to annihilate the very form it is able to receive or create ... to talk about the plasticity of the brain means to see in it not only the creator and receiver of form but also an agency of disobedience to every constituted form, a refusal to submit to a model.[15]

In *The Future of Hegel*, Malabou links the Greek *hexis* (habit) with *exein* (to have/possess): seizing control of our own plasticity enables a liberating form of self-possession and also (perhaps conversely) invites new habits to 'possess' us until we find it hard to change them, coming to will them of our own accord.[16] Malabou's work illuminates the ways in which Thomas resisted mainstream social norms and reshaped himself by habituating himself to Quaker patterns of behaviour that ultimately guided his inmost thoughts. Simultaneously, as I discuss below, other forms of self-shaping are in play in *The History* as Thomas constructs and affirms his manly, class-conscious identity through his prose.

Malabou's work speaks well to early modern writing because she builds on Aristotelian ideas about habit and plastic power (or 'virtue') that informed early modern thought. The very phrase 'plastic power' is a seventeenth-century phrase; for seventeenth-century writers, 'plastic power' combines the ensouled body's physiological ability to heal itself and develop into a distinct shape, and the 'plastic' art of sculpture (I discuss the latter's aesthetic connotations below).[17] Malabou summarises, 'plasticity . . . also means the ability to evolve and adapt. It is this sense we invoke when we speak of a "plastic virtue" possessed by animals, plants, and, in general, all living things'.[18] Though they tend to associate plasticity with humans' lower, material nature, as opposed to the superior spiritual aspect of their being, early modern writers often describe physiological plasticity affecting a person's temperament. For the natural philosopher Joseph Glanvill (1636–80), plastic power is mysteriously uncertain, 'what it is, how it works, and whose it is, we cannot learn . . . For though the Soul be supposed to be the Bodies Maker, and the builder of its own house; yet by what kind of Knowledge, Method, or Means, is as unknown'.[19] Malabou draws on neuroscience to explain what stumped Glanvill: how the soul can be the 'builder of its own house'. She states that, when we decisively choose or refuse to behave according to a particular mode of life, our synapses and wider physiology destroy, strengthen, and (re)generate forms and modes of behaviour.

Much Quaker literature cautions against too much exposure to worldly milieux and mainstream society as this might weaken desirable Quaker habits and induce conformity to Anglican practices. Writers advise Quakers to spend time alone or with other Quakers, in order to focus on developing and strengthening Quaker behaviour. Thereby, God permeates the Quaker's inner life, shaping them from within; they align their will with God's. Opponents of Quakerism criticised this introspective self-shaping as blasphemous and narcissistic. Former Quaker turned Quaker nemesis Francis Bugg's 1704 broadside *The Character of a Quaker*, argues that Quakers sacrilegiously presumed to 'mould' God himself, 'He [the Quaker] casts Christianity in the *mould* of his Fancy

... Believes in a Christ Conceiv'd, Born, Crucified, and raised from the dead WITHIN him'.[20] In the latter half of the seventeenth century, Mary and Isaac Penington's daughter (also named Mary Penington) transcribes into her commonplace book several of Fox's precepts about how Quakerism 'keeps it self from the spotts of the world' by eschewing and rejecting 'the Worlds Manners & fashions'.[21] From the beginning of *The History*, Thomas is aware of the effects of his milieu on his personal spiritual development. When young, he writes, he 'preserved' his developing soul and personality from 'Prophaneness' that might infect his character:

> I always sorted myself with Persons of Ingenuity, Temperance and sobriety for I loathed Scurrilities in Conversation, and had a natural Aversion to immoderate Drinking. So I was preserved from Prophaneness and the grosser Evils of the World, which rendered me acceptable to persons of the best Note.[22]

'Persons of the best Note' indicates that Thomas sought to habituate himself to behaviours valued by upper-class society, as well as 'preserv[ing]' his morals. Walter's commands to go to (and stay in) his chamber, and sicknesses caused by Walter beating him and stealing his hat in winter, frequently confine Thomas to his room. Thomas uses this solitude to foster radical piety, imagining himself developing from a seed God has planted. On one occasion, he expresses this in poetry; buds of two metrical feet surge with sap and flower into a third foot, like Thomas' Quaker piety blooming in his solitude

> The Winter Tree
> Resembles me,
>   Whose Sap lies in its Root:
> The Spring draws nigh;
>   As it, so I
> Shall bud, I hope, and shoot.[23]

In perfect masculine rhyme, Thomas neatly figures his solitude as a constructive development towards, and in alignment with, God. As we shall continue to see, Thomas's interactions with other people reveal classed and gendered elements to his self-shaping that sometimes run counter to this tidy Quaker project.

Malabou contrasts plasticity, whereby the human subject takes control of their self-shaping, with 'flexibility' whereby the subject passively allows other people to mould them. Flexible bodies are, like Foucauldian 'docile bodies', disempowered by their malleability: so completely primed to desire what the state desires and enact the state's commands that they have no energy remaining, or capacity to conceive of ways of knowing and being outside the framework provided by the state. As a result, their experience of their 'autonomy' in fact involves participation in the institutions that control them.[24] Malabou writes that whereas plasticity involves 'rupture and resistance' – the ability to create form, destroy old forms that no longer serve us, and resist unwanted shaping – flexibility is purely passive and 'conciliatory'.[25] Flexibility is,

> only one of the semantic registers of plasticity: that of receiving form. To be flexible is to receive a form or impression, to be able to fold oneself, to take the fold, not to give it. To be docile, to not explode. Indeed, what flexibility lacks is the resource of giving form, the power to create, to invent or even to erase an impression, the power to style. Flexibility is plasticity minus its genius.[26]

Thomas is keenly aware of the difference between consciously shaping his life according to moral principles he has chosen for himself, and passively allowing authorities to mould him into whatever form they want. Another short creative piece he includes in *The History* is a dialogue between a Bishop ('B') and a Quaker ('Q') about conformity, in response to laws prohibiting Quaker meetings. The Bishop wants worshippers to be what Malabou calls 'flexible': obediently conforming to whatever albeit random dictates the Bishop issues. The Quaker, conversely, is 'conformable' only to 'the Image of the Son': not allowing 'fickle' authorities to mould them, but thoughtfully cultivating a Christlike life,

> CONFORMITY *Prest and Represt*
> B. *WHAT! You are one of them that do deny*
> *To yield Obedience by Conformity.*
> Q. Nay: We desire conformable to be.
> B. *But unto what?* Q. The Image of the Son.
> B. *What's that to us! We'll have Conformity*
> *Unto our Form.* Q. Then we shall ne'er have done,
> For if your fickle Minds should alter,
> We should be to seek a New Conformity.
> This who To-day conform to *Prelacy*,
> To-morrow may conform to *Popery*.
> But take this for an Answer, *Bishop*, we
> Cannot conform either to them, or Thee.[27]

The Quaker refuses to be what the Bishop wants them to be: putty in Bishops' hands. With typical Quaker logic, Thomas's Quaker argues that, through being a religious 'non-conformist', they are in fact the most 'conformable' Christian because they closely conform to Christ's image.

Malabou emphasises the importance of being conscious of how our selfhood is shaped through habits and externally-imposed ideologies so that we can seize control of the shaping process. Quakers like Thomas Ellwood plastically adapted their lives to avoid simply thoughtlessly submitting to (and thus being moulded by) mainstream religious and social norms. Quakers were aware of the ways in which hat-doffing, deferent language, saying grace, Christian Sabbath rules, swearing oaths, and church ceremonies produced obedient Anglican subjects. Refusing to participate in these behaviours, they adhered instead to a non-conformist pattern of behaviour. Thomas's writing is part of his Quaker way of life: he plastically shapes himself into a Quaker author and his prose moulds his thoughts and deeds to fit an unadorned, truthful-seeming Quaker writing style. In *The History*, as he remembers the heady days of his youth, the weight of his body slows the prose and demands to be admired. Conscious of his class status, moreover, Thomas often carefully depicts his interactions with men of Walter's class as conversations between equals. As we saw in the previous chapter, seduced by his own youthful high spirits, Guzmán struggled to write a moralising story about his younger escapades. Thomas offers a non-fiction, English non-conformist version of these struggles of life-writing, wherein his classed and gendered consciousness of his body at times warps his Quaker message and at others informs his construction of his manly Quaker identity.

'Peace and Quietness'? Thomas Ellwood's Literary Shaping of His Life

Through *The History*, Thomas shapes an aesthetic self. His body and will, which he tries to align with God's, drive his shaping of both his text and (often together with) his Quaker self. His body and spirited will also challenge his prose's plainness and its sense of calm honesty and reflective conscience so lauded by Quaker stylists. Attention to *The History*'s literary qualities elucidates the specifically aesthetic dimension of the soul's 'plastic power'. Since the first (plentiful) use of the word 'plasticke' in English by Richard Haydock in his 1598 translation of G. P. Lomazzo's work, *A Tracte Containing the Arts of Curious Painting, Carving and Building*, 'plasticity' suggests sculpting, shaping, and moulding our own personalities and brains as if we are a work of art. Haydock's Preface states, 'God was the first Plasticke worker' because 'with his owne hande hee framed the moulde of the first man and afterwards most miraculously inspired it with a living soule'.[28] Drawing on the Greek etymology (*plassein*: to mould), Malabou describes the brain as a work-in-progress of 'plastic organic art', akin to 'sculpture, modelling, architecture'.[29] Malabou is attentive to the ways in which cultural and social factors (re)form the brain more broadly, however this metaphor of the plastic arts in particular pervasively guides and informs her conceptualisation of plasticity: for example, she describes the normal process of neuronal death as 'the sculptor's chisel' creating form.[30] Malabou compares the brain's ability to retain the imprints of new forms to sculpture: we often find 'there is no possible return to the indeterminacy of the starting point', just as, she writes, a block of marble sculpted into a statue cannot return to its original block-shape.[31] Several – sometimes antagonistic – shaping forces are at play in *The History*, giving the text its form: Thomas's wider English society, his family, his body and will, God's shaping power over his life and his Quaker milieu.

Thomas wrote creatively and appreciated poetry, including short creative works in *The History* as we have seen, publishing further occasional poems and a 1712 epic on King David (*Davideis*). He also claimed to have inspired Milton's *Paradise Regained*. In her essay on Quaker literature, Nancy Jiwon Cho explains that many early Quakers viewed creative writing as 'deceitful, profane or vain': 'early Friends believed that writing should be simple and honest—and, consequently, that artful genres were at best frivolous and at worst diabolical'.[32] Early Quaker creative writing was rare and, when, as in Thomas's case, it did exist, authors often deliberately left metre, form, and vocabulary unpolished. Cho details how early Quakers valued truth and conscience over elegant writing, emphasising that the writing should eschew fiction, involving no 'artifice or invention'.[33] Cho demonstrates that though the earliest Quakers understood 'the power of the written word' and that 'writing could be a tool for the forging of the fledgling movement's identity', they focused on writing in a way that was sober, plain, and honest, and were cautioned by Fox only to write when moved by God. Cho explains that early Quakers numbered 'nonfictional prose' like *The History*, and journals like Mary Penington's among the more acceptable forms of writing, as they were associated with these desired qualities.[34] In *The History*, Thomas eschews varied, abstruse vocabulary and bombastic use of rhetorical devices for their own sake, to present an unimpeachable Quaker narrative. Thomas's friend the Quaker Joseph Wyeth's Preface to *The History* describes Thomas as an exemplary Quaker prose stylist. Wyeth edited *The History* and added a 'supplement' to it, continuing Thomas's life where Thomas left off in 1683 and defending Thomas's treatment of Walter against his critics. Wyeth invites the reader to consider whether they are conscientious and 'judicious' enough to appreciate Thomas's style which is learned but not in a pretentious way, devoted primarily to the plain truth:

> *the judicious Reader will easily observe, that his Method and Stile do denote him to have been a Scholar: And yet not farther so, than the Simplicity and Purity of the* Truth, *whereof he made Profession, would permit him.*[35]

Quakers associated simple and plain prose with truthfulness and good conscience. Writing in this recognisably Quaker style thus lends authority to Thomas's writing as it implies that he wrote with radical Christian emphasis on eliminating lies, malice, and pride.

Thomas's 'Simplicity and Purity' are refracted through a class- and gender-conscious lens. As Nigel Smith notes, the professional, artisanal, and merchant classes were overrepresented in seventeenth-century radical religion.[36] Thanks to the privileges they enjoyed as members of such classes, (relatively) socially-high-ranking Quakers like Thomas had an investment in social hierarchy that made their rejections of it ambiguous. In *A Retrospective Glass for the Quakers* (1710), Bugg describes Quakers 'pretending they cannot seek to Outward Authority, when no people on Earth seek more to Outward Authority than they do'.[37] When a Justice examines Thomas along with several other Quakers who had gathered together in a meeting that to outsiders had niffed of sedition and plots, Thomas connects with the official through shared knowledge of upper class society:

> He asked me many Questions, concerning my Birth, my Education, my Acquaintance in *Oxfordshire;* particularly what Men of Note I knew there. To all which I gave him brief, but plain and true Answers; naming several Families, of the best Rank, in that Part of the Country where I dwelt . . .[38]

Thomas's style of speaking and writing is 'plain and true', and 'brief' rather than elaborate, however the content of what he says alludes to and bolsters his social status. Thomas's frankness serves a purpose other than furthering the Quaker cause: it enables him to connect with the Justice as an equal, to network with him as a member of a similar social class.

Though as we have seen (and will continue to see) he carefully crafted his point of view to Walter's detriment and to the advantage of both himself and the Quaker cause, Thomas's prose style implies that his viewpoint is synonymous with the Christ-approved truth. Quakers sought to achieve what Smith describes as a *'merging* [of] the self with the One Light', aligning their thoughts and behaviour with God's will.[39] Quaker writing, too, aligns persecuted Quakers with Christ, and their tormentors with Christ's tormentors. Suffering violence was common in Quaker writings: 'Oh, the daily reproaches and beatings in highways because we would not put off our hats: and for saying "thou" to people', exclaims Fox.[40] The anonymous author of 'A Paper shewing how the Servants of the Lord was beaten as they are now' rehearses various biblical precedents (including the beating of Christ himself) to align Quaker victims of violence with scripture's righteous victims.⁴¹ Another paper collected with it adduces the actions of historical saints, disruptors like Jeremiah, and Christ overturning the moneylenders' tables to emphasise that Quakers follow laudable models in breaking with the customs of the world.⁴² Though society condemned Quaker behaviour as irreligious and disruptive to society, these writings argue that it is the Quakers' persecutors who are, by biblical standards, in fact the most badly behaved. By casting themselves and their opponents into the mould of biblical precedent, the Quakers emphasised the enduring nature of the textual and behavioural patterns they fit themselves into. Even when recollecting passionate and distressing encounters with Walter, *The History* coolly presents both the young Thomas (who experienced the encounter) and the older Thomas (who records the encounter in writing) as calmly Christ-like. Suffering Walter's retributive blows for calling Walter 'Thou' rather than 'You', Thomas does not retaliate with physical violence but arrests Walter's hand mid-attack by asking 'if God should serve thee so, when thou sayest Thou or Thee to him?'.⁴³ Walter then retreats, and Thomas retires to his chamber to pray.

Thomas's plain, calm writing with its Christlike emphasis on enduring torments without retaliating violently, can lead to somewhat detached and dispassionate descriptions of his body. When, following Thomas's lead, the Ellwood household servants stop attending family prayers, Walter hits Thomas repeatedly with a cane, wounding the arm Thomas raises to protect his head. Thomas relates that Walter is so carried away that he only stops beating Thomas when Thomas's sister cries out that she fears Thomas will die. Thomas's response is coolly, meekly Quaker:

> my Sister followed me to see my Arm and dress it, for it was indeed very much bruised and swelled between the Wrist and the Elbow; and in some Places the Skin was broken and beaten off. But though it was very sore, and I felt for some Time much Pain in it, yet I had Peace and Quietness in my Mind, being more grieved for my Father than for myself, who I knew had hurt himself more than me.⁴⁴

Thomas's initial description of his wounds does not tie his clearly painful arm to emotions; with clinical detachment, he details the damage to his arm, 'much bruised and swelled between the Wrist and the Elbow; and in some Places the Skin was broken and beaten off'. He does not express anger (quite the reverse, he feels 'Peace'); with Christlike altruism, the only grief he admits to is grief for Walter's soul. Later, Walter steals Thomas's hat because he cannot bear to see Thomas refusing to doff it. 'Laid up as a kind of Prisoner', sick and cold for lack of a hat, Thomas matter-of-factly describes his bodily pain:

> This was in the eleventh month, called *January*, and the Weather sharp; so that I, who had been bred more tenderly, took so great a Cold in my Head that my Face and Head were much swelled; and my Gums had on them Boils so sore, that I could neither chew Meat, nor without difficulty swallow Liquids. It held long, and I underwent much Pain, without much Pity, except from my poor Sister, who did what she could to give me Ease; and at length, by frequent Applications of Figs and stoned Raisins toasted, and laid to the Boyls as hot as I could bear them, they ripened fit for lancing, and soon after sunk; then I had Ease.[45]

Thomas largely evacuates his text of anger and rancorous blame against Walter, focusing instead on bodily pain, the mechanics of eating, and the process of 'ripen[ing]' boils with toasted fruits. Nevertheless, Thomas's unflinching depiction of his own sore and swollen head, face, and mouth points towards Walter, whose refusal to allow Thomas a hat surely caused this 'great ... Cold'.

Thomas emphasises his own clear conscience in contrast to Walter's self-destructive behaviour. In so doing, Thomas posits himself as a pattern that his readers should follow; he states early on that he hopes 'others, whose lot it may be to tread the same path and fall into the same or like exercises, may be encouraged to persevere in the way of holiness'.[46] His writing suggests that his thoughts and lifestyle were imbued with Christic simplicity. However, as I now go on to discuss, at other times Thomas's body troubles 'the *Simplicity and Purity of the* Truth'.

Masculinity and Self-Shaping: A Simple Perspective?

In her study of gender and social class in (the senior) Mary Penington's and Thomas Ellwood's life-writing, Naomi Baker deduces 'unresolved tensions' between these Quakers' snobbish consciousness of their high social rank and Quakerism's disrespect of social hierarchies. Baker sees Thomas grappling with this issue as his constructs an 'anxiously' chivalrous and class-conscious masculinity,

> Ellwood's autobiography anxiously negotiates with the masculine subject positions that are undermined by both his unstable social position and his Quaker identity. Ellwood's social and gendered insecurity in fact generates a more acute defensiveness and reticence in his self-representation than is apparent in Penington's life writing.[47]

Heeding Thomas's contemporaries who accused him of 'converting to Quakerism merely in order to secure a high social position', Baker suggests that he used Quakerism for social advancement, concluding that when it came to rejecting social hierarchies he and Mary Penington 'are never fully at ease with this aspect of their religious identity' and that 'after numerous social humiliations, Quakerism is therefore presented as the one means by which Ellwood can succeed in the opinion of those who (in his eyes at least) are "above" him'.[48] By attaching himself to the high-ranking Penington family, and emulating the gentlemanly manliness of its patriarch Isaac Penington, Thomas 'could re-negotiate the negative implications of a Quaker identity'.[49] Complementing Baker's analysis of social status in *The History*, I am interested in how Thomas shows his manly power though the physicality of his body. Boiling blood, nimble movements, and youthful strength and stamina suggest the vigour that drives and sustains Thomas's writing and resistance to behavioural norms, but also disorganises his claims to a humble, non-violent Quaker identity. By invoking his body as a source of Quaker suffering and tenacity, Thomas brings more gendered bodily concerns into play. Both experienced in his body, his Quaker endurance of pain and his manly stamina blend into one. The effect is exacerbated because he uses much of the same vocabulary to describe Quaker suffering and displays of physical strength. At times, his desire to impress his superior physical strength onto his readers leads him away from immediate Quaker concerns (like humility, non-violence, the doctrine of equality), demonstrating the body's unruliness and enmeshment in a variety of frames of reference (class, gender, sectarian religion) without being reducible to a single one.

At several points in *The History*, Thomas engages in physical combat, slowing down to unpick his victories blow by blow. Describing how he conquered two thieves who waylaid him and Walter on the road before he became a Quaker, Thomas ensures that his readers do not miss a single key bodily movement,

> my Father, turning his Head to me, said, TOM, *disarm them*.
>
> I stood ready at his Elbow, waiting only for the Word of Command. For being naturally of a bold Spirit, full then of youthful Heat, and that too heightened by the Sense I had, not only for the Abuse, but insolent Behaviour of those rude Fellows; my Blood began to boil, and my Fingers itch'd, as the Saying is, to be dealing with them. Wherefore stepping boldly forward, to lay hold on the Staff of him that was nearest to me, I said, *Sirrah, deliver your Weapon*. He thereupon raised his Club, which was big enough to have knockt down an Ox, intending no doubt to have knockt me down with it, as probably he would have done, had I not, in the Twinkling of an Eye, whipt out my Rapier and made a Pass upon him. I could not have failed running of him through up to the Hilt, had he stood his Ground; but the suddain and unexpected Sight of my bright Blade, glistering in the dark Night, did so amaze and terrify the Man, that slipping aside, he avoided my Thrust, and letting his Staff sink, betook himself to his Heels for Safety, which his Companion seeing, fled also. I followed the former as fast as I could, but *Timor addidit*

> *Alas*, Fear gave him Wings, and made him swiftly fly, so that although I was accounted very nimble, yet the farther we ran, the more Ground he gain'd on me, so that I could not overtake him.⁵⁰

Though Thomas emphasises the speed of the fight (he reacted to the danger 'in the Twinkling of an Eye', his sword-arm's reflex 'suddain', the subsequent pursuit 'swift', 'nimble', and as if winged), he describes it as if it occurs in slow motion. Thereby, he dwells on his body in interaction with the robbers'. In the moment, he responded to the raised club by drawing his rapier 'in the Twinkling of an Eye'; recounting this moment, Thomas slows down the narrative to dwell on the looming club. Between the raised club, and the whipt-out Rapier, he interpolates a four-clause-long drawn-out contemplation of the club's size, the clues it gives Thomas about the robber's intention, and the painful future it offers Thomas: 'He thereupon raised his Club, which was big enough to have knockt down an Ox, intending no doubt to have knockt me down with it, as probably he would have done, had I not, in the Twinkling of an Eye, whipt out my Rapier'. 'Sink' is an oddly slow verb for what in fact seems to have happened rapidly, especially as Thomas has just emphasised the club's weight (making it more likely to plummet quickly towards the ground rather than slowly 'sink'): seeing Thomas draw his rapier, the robber lets his heavy club fall and scarpers. The odd word 'sink' and the *paulatim* description in which it is embedded, lead readers to pause and imagine the club slowly drooping in contradistinction to Thomas's brilliantly superior 'bright Blade ... glistering'. Thomas simultaneously unpacks his quick instinctive thinking, evokes the hyper-alert state of a person in danger who notices every detail around them, and emphasises the size of his opponent's weapon and thereby his own valour: implicitly, he is as brave as if he were bigger than a hefty Ox.

In this episode Thomas is his father's attack dog, 'itch[ing]' to spring at Walter's command. This encounter with the robber is peculiarly similar to a later encounter in which Thomas detaches himself from Walter, the quotation with which I opened this book:

> observing that my Father gained Ground upon me, I somewhat mended my Pace. This he observing, mended his Pace also; and at length Ran. Whereupon I ran also; and a fair Course we had, through a large Meadow of his, which lay behind his House and of sight of the Town. He was not, I suppose, then above Fifty Years of Age; and being light of Body, and nimble of Foot, he held to it for a while. But afterwards slacking his Pace to take Breath, and observing that I had gotten Ground of him; he turned back, and went home.⁵¹

Reading this passage alongside the description of the robber with his club shows Thomas jumbling subject-positions; in the chase with Walter, sometimes Thomas, and sometimes Walter evokes the escaping robber. 'This he observing, mended his Pace also' and 'which his Companion seeing, fled also' are similar fragments of prose: each combines a relative clause with the use of 'also' after a verb of movement, moreover the overall sense of both fragments is similar: one man sees another run and runs likewise. As Thomas chases the robber and gives up, Thomas reflects 'yet the farther we ran, the more Ground he gain'd on me so that I could not overtake him'; later, Thomas is the fleet-footed escapee gaining ground on Walter: 'observing that I had gotten Ground of him; he turned back, and went home'. Both Thomas and the robber are 'nimble'. Reusing vocabulary, clause-structure, and ideas in these two passages, Thomas suggests that his flight from his father is a display of youthful manly spirit like his fight with the robbers. In making he and Walter inconsistently evoke both the robber and the better-armed pursuer, Thomas blurs boundaries between right and wrong. Who, out of he and Walter, is chasing and who is fleeing? Is the pursuer a violent father or the victor in a fight? Is the fleeing man a wicked thief or a righteous Quaker?

Reflecting, Thomas questions whether squaring up to the robber was the best idea. In a tone of honest confession, he explains that he was initially pleased with his 'Bravery' and remained in a bloodthirsty mood for some time, but ultimately concludes that his behaviour serves best as a warning for how *not* to behave: 'I have given this Account of that Action, that others may be warned by it'.[52] He writes, 'for a good while after, I had no Regrets upon my Mind for what I had done, and designed to have done, in this Case; but went on in a sort of Bravery, resolving to kill, if I could, any man that should make the like Attempt, or put any Affront upon us', however when God took him 'out of the Spirit and Ways of the World', 'a sort of Horror seized on me when I considered how near I had been to the staining of my Hands with human blood'.[53] Though Thomas retrospectively condemns the way he behaved with the robber, his description has already led his reader's attention to linger on his body and its hot-tempered strength. The plainness of his style has already enforced connections between his chase with the robber and his chase with Walter: repeated vocabulary and sentence-structures are key to the unadorned way Thomas writes, creating resonances between different episodes in *The History*. As a result, he describes encounters with very different men in similar terms. This continues beyond the two passages I have just cited. For example, when Thomas challenges Walter, 'if God should serve thee so, when thou sayest Thou or Thee to him?', Walter's hand, like the robber's club, 'sinks'.[54] Now Thomas's non-violent, righteous words are 'bright' and 'glistering', taking the place of his rapier in an antagonistic encounter with another man.

Thomas deploys this way of writing about his body when describing his life both before and after his turn to Quakerism. After being 'convinced' as a Quaker, he relates another slowed-down violent encounter when he saves Giuli Penington from 'A Knot' of men 'designing ... to put an Abuse upon us, and make themselves Sport with us'.[55] Thomas positions this as a matter of the men's jealousy of his and Giuli's high social class, 'the *Roysters* ... grudged us both the Horses we rode, and the Cloaths we wore'.[56] As he and Giuli ride abreast chatting, Thomas recounts,

> on a sudden hearing a little Noise, and turning mine Eye that Way, I saw an Horseman coming up on the further side of her Horse, having his left Arm stretched out, just ready to take her about the Waste, and pluck her off backwards from her own Horse, to lay her before him upon his. I had but just Time to thrust forth my Stick between him and her, and bid him stand off; and at the same Time reigning my Horse, to let hers go before me, thrust in between her and him, and being better mounted than he, my Horse run him off. But his Horse being (tho' weaker than mine, yet) nimble, he slipt by me, and got up to her on the near Side, endeavouring to offer Abuse to her: To prevent which, I thrust in upon him again, and in our jostling, we drove her Horse quite out the Way, and almost into the next Hedge.[57]

By picking apart actions that happened simultaneously (thrusting his stick between the attacker and Giuli, telling the attacker to 'stand off', and reigning in his horse) and describing them one after another, Thomas draws out what was originally another quick-fire encounter. Though Thomas rapidly interprets and responds to his attacker's malevolent intentions, Giuli's perspective is absent from the narrative; Thomas does not take Giuli's thoughts or reactions into account. Giuli's horse is more active than she is; indeed the horses come to dominate the interactions: Thomas states that he allowed Giuli's horse (presumably with Giuli on it) to move in front rather than representing Giuli as taking any initiative. In the final sentence quoted above, Thomas and the attacker seem weirdly united in their attack on Giuli's horse, 'in our jostling, we drove her Horse quite out the Way, and almost into the next Hedge'. Giuli is an inert body on a horse: plucked, bent backwards, her trajectory altered when her horse is jostled along without the jostlers seeming to worry about unseating her. Despite Giuli's passivity, the description enables us to infer features of her body: Giuli was light and compact enough to be picked up with one arm (the avian word 'plucked' suggests feather-lightness), flexible enough to be bent or drawn backwards from her horse, and a good horse rider who can withstand the jostling (presumably Thomas would have noted if Giuli had fallen off). The telling gaps in Thomas's account of the assault highlight the fact that Thomas only gives us his own, particular, perspective. Perhaps Giuli did fight the attacker off, and control her own horse, but these details did not fit the narrative Thomas desired to write. Despite his esteem for Giuli, when Thomas slows down to contemplate his physical and moral victory against another man, he 'jostles' his woman companion to the side.

Thomas relies on many of the same movement-words to describe all the physical encounters I have discussed in this section. Repeating words like 'nimble', 'sink', and 'thrust' suggests that, in his plain descriptions of bodily movement, Thomas does not dwell precisely and minutely on the body, preferring to keep his mind on spiritual matters. In fact, however, Thomas's pure and simple style frequently follows the kinaesthetic melodies of his and other people's bodies blow by blow, clause by clause. Though his style is associated with truthfulness, his is not a neutral perspective. Rather, in his focus on his body in chase and combat with other men's, Thomas elides Giuli's viewpoint and troubles the neat moral division between himself and Walter. Cognitive cultural theorists often highlight the importance of cognition and plasticity as a process, from Bolens emphasising (as we saw in the Introduction) 'sensorimotor interaction' to Malabou stating that plasticity is not simply a quality of ourselves: it *is* our very selves: 'Being is nothing but its plasticity'.[58] Bruce McConachie writes that though 'mind' is officially a noun, it can be better to think of it as a verb: the mind is interactive and generative.[59] *The History* tracks and (re)creates the processes whereby Thomas works out his gendered, classed, sectarian identity through the kinaesthetic melody of his body in interaction with others'.

Authentic Shaping, Fake Pliancy: Thomas and the False Quakers

Thomas contrasts his deep and authentic personal development with the chameleonic self-shaping of people who pretend, for devious reasons, to be Quakers. People pretending to be Quakers begin to infiltrate the Quaker movement from its earliest decades, attempting to gain incriminating personal details about Quakers that could cause their downfalls. Thomas relates,

> in some Parts of the Nation Care had been taken, by some not of the lowest Rank, to chuse out some particular Persons (Men of sharp Wit, close Countenances, pliant Tempers, and deep Dissimulation) and send them forth among the *Sectaries*, so called; with Instructions to thrust themselves into all Societies, conform to all, or any Sort of religious Profession, *Proteus*-like change their Shapes, and transform themselves from one religious

Appearance to another, as Occasion should require. In a Word, to be all Things to all; not that they might win some, but that they might, if possible, ruin all, at least many.[60]

The Proteus-like transformation of these dissimulating false Quakers contrasts with Thomas's radical plasticity. The infiltrators' 'pliant Tempers' involve them in only the most superficial shaping. By contrast, Thomas's Quaker identity also involves what Malabou calls the 'constancy' needed to retain the form of life one has chosen. One false Quaker is easily revealed as his pliancy is no match for the rigours of a sober, simple, and truthful Quaker pattern of life; though he superficially conforms to Quaker behaviours, his unruly drunken nature soon bursts forth. He,

> thrust himself upon a Friend, under the counterfeit Appearance of a *Quaker*; but being by the Friend suspected, and thereupon dismist unentertain'd, he was forced to betake himself to an Inn or Alehouse for Accommodation. Long he had not been there, e're his unruly Nature (not to be long kept under by the Curb of a feigned Sobriety) broke forth into open Profaneness.[61]

Thomas works to tame his own boiling blood, nimble legs, and itching fingers in the service of profound and lasting Quaker self-shaping. By contrast, the counterfeit Quaker's supposedly Quaker behaviour is a mere veneer through which his 'Profaneness' soon 'broke forth'.

In prison, Thomas meets another man who pretends to be a Quaker; this man does so in order to get arrested and then scrounge imprisoned Quakers' food. Presumably, the false Quaker is penurious enough to make this an attractive option for him. Thomas (who, though starving, had previously abstained from food freely offered by other Quakers in prison) shows little empathy for this 'shabby fellow', though, capping his description of the false Quaker's behaviour with an abstract fable of a Drone and Bees,

> Whenever he saw any Victuals brought forth for them to eat, he would be sure to thrust in with Knife in Hand, and make himself his own Carver; and so impudent was he, that if he saw the provision was short, whatever he wanted, he would be sure to take enough.
>
> Thus lives this lazy Drone upon the Labours of the industrious Bees, to his high Content and their no small Trouble, to whom his Company was as offensive, as his Ravening was oppressive.[62]

When the prisoners are gathered together to be sorted into new prison quarters, the 'lazy Drone' puts on a Quaker show for the sheriff, attempting to ensure that he is kept with the Quakers (and their food). Thomas thwarts the false Quaker's plan, 'he . . . thrust himself amongst us . . . I saw him standing there with his Hat on, and looking as demurely as he could, that the sheriff might take him for a *Quaker*; At Sight of which, my spirit was much stirred'; Thomas tells the sheriff this man is 'no Quaker but an idle dissolute Fellow'.[63] Celebrating remorselessly, Thomas relates that the sheriff locks the man up with the Felons instead, 'and so Friends had a good Deliverance of him'.[64] Like the drunken infiltrator, this false Quaker instantly renounces the superficial Quaker patterns of behaviour he had adopted when they no longer serve him; he removes his hat and bows to the Sheriff as he pleads in deferent language to be either released or put with the Quakers.

Thomas's treatment of the Felons is similarly two-dimensional; just as the false Quaker is an idle drone, the felons are felonious through and through. However, Thomas's plain style with its reused vocabulary complicates the distinction between true and false Quakers by generating congruences between Thomas's bodily movements and the bodily movements of the very people he is concerned to distinguish himself from. As the false Quakers 'thrust' themselves among true Quakers in meetings and prison cells, and the kidnappers 'thrust' in between Thomas and Giuli, Thomas 'thrust' himself among the kidnappers and threatens the robbers with a 'Thrust'. Disparate characters engage in similar acts of kinesis in *The History*; as bodies repeatedly shove each other, their opposition begins to look like similarity. Smith refers to the Quakers' 'fierce enthusiasm' for God which resulted in 'violent language'.[65] Thomas's 'violent language' crystallises around antagonistic encounters with other people, however; even in a plain and simple style of writing, the body comes complexly to the fore. Thomas draws on his body – both its vigour and its capacity for suffering – to resist his father and the more mundane assaults of the world. His body in prose also complicates the relationship between Thomas's social station, Quakerism, and his gendered relationships with others.

Conclusion

Thomas shapes his Quaker identity in alignment with God. His body is part of that shaping, and Thomas develops, tests, and consolidates his Quaker identity through embodied interactions with others. As prose is part of that shaping, prose tangles Thomas's body with others' in ways that at times emphasise violent kinesis over moral distinctions between Quakers and non-Quakers. Malabou describes necessary contradictions between opposing 'energies': fluidity and rigidity, resistance and pliancy, destroying old forms and relationships and creating new ones. *The History* is a space where these contradictions appear; *The History* is also created through these contradictions. It is a record and product of Thomas's plasticity and it forms part of his plastic self-shaping. Three centuries later, it holds part of the Quaker form he has created alongside traces of his pre-Quaker way of life.

Notes

1. Ellwood, *The History*, D3v.
2. Ellwood, *The History*, D3v. On hat honour see Susan Wareham Watkins, 'Hat Honour, Self-Identity and Commitment in Early Quakerism', *Quaker History* 103(1) (2014) (1–16), 1–2; George Fox, *Concerning Good-morrow and good-even* (London: for Thomas Simmons, 1657), B4v; Richard Hubberthorne, 'Doffing hats worse then [sic] a heathenish vanity' in *A True Testimony of the zeal of Oxford Professors and University Men* (London: for Giles Calvert, 1654), B1r-v. A lively example of Quaker opposition to hat honour is William Dewsbury refusing to remove his hat in court; Anon, *A Discovery of the ground from which the Persecution did arise* (London, [s.n.]: 1655), A4v.
3. Thomas records several ways Walter disadvantaged his life, such as removing him from school (where Thomas was a promising scholar) in order to pay for his older brother's studies in Oxford and retracting his offer of money when Thomas contracts a Quaker marriage. With quiet delight, Thomas describes Walter attempting to argue with Quakers about religion and the Quakers coming off better, *The History*, D2r.
4. See Robynne Rogers Healey, 'History of Quaker Faith and Practice 1650–1808', in Stephen Angell and Pink Dandelion, eds, *The Cambridge Companion to Quakerism* (Cambridge: Cambridge University Press, 2018) (13–30), 15.
5. Herman Roodenberg notes that Quakers had no problem with egalitarian gestures like handshakes, which enabled them to show respect and warm affection without granting to humans the subordination reserved for God, 'The hand of friendship: shaking hands and other gestures in the Dutch Republic', in Jan Bremmer and Herman Roodenburg, eds, *A Cultural History of Gesture* (Cornell University Press, 1991), (152–89), 153, 176.
6. George Fox, *A Warning to England* (London: s.n., 1674), [unsigned fols] fol 3v.
7. R. H., *The Character of a Quaker* (London: for T Egglesfield, 1671), B3v. See Nicholas Jagger, 'Austin, Samuel (*fl.* 1652–1671)', *Oxford Dictionary of National Biography* (2004) [online] https://doi.org/10.1093/ref:odnb/914 [last accessed 08.11.2019]. Responding anonymously to Thomas Ellwood's writings, the clergyman and later Dean of Durham Thomas Comber wrote that the Quaker 'will neither Preach nor Pray, nor say Grace when he sitteth down to meat', *Christianity No Enthusiasm* (London: T. D., 1678), B4r.
8. Aristotle, *Nichomachean Ethics*, trans. H. Rackham (Cambridge, MA: Harvard University Press, 1926), 2.35.
9. Ramie Targoff, *Common Prayer: The Language of Devotion in Early Modern England* (Carolina: Carolina University Press, 2001), 4.

10. Ellwood, *The History*, C1v.
11. Ellwood, *The History*, C2r-v.
12. Neuroscientist Mark Jeannerod explains that habitually using certain synapses (structures which allow electrical signals to pass between nerve cells) when we perform certain actions and have certain thoughts strengthens those synapses and increases their responsiveness. Rarely-used synapses become increasingly less responsive. This results in 'the gradual molding of a brain under the influence of individual experience', cited in Catherine Malabou, *What Should We Do with Our Brain?*, trans. Sebastian Rand (New York: Fordham University Press, 2008), 7. For my earlier discussion of Malabou and plasticity see Laura Seymour, 'Doth Not Brutus Bootless Kneel? Kneeling, Cognition and Destructive Plasticity in Shakespeare's *Julius Caesar*', *Theatre, Performance and Cognition* (40–53), 45–8.
13. Catherine Malabou, *The Future of Hegel: Plasticity, Temporality, and Dialectic*, trans. Lisabeth During (London: Routledge, 2005), 24–6, 76, 32, 57l; cf. Malabou, *What Should We Do with Our Brain?*, 71. Malabou restates this in later work, arguing that we live 'between an excess of reification and an excess of fluidification'. Catherine Malabou, *Plasticity at the Dusk of Writing*, trans. Caroline Shread (Columbia: Columbia University Press, 2010), 81.
14. Malabou, *The Future of Hegel*, 70–1.
15. Malabou, *What Should We Do with Our Brain?*, 5.
16. Malabou, *The Future of Hegel*, 37–8, 56. Malabou writes, 'habit is the process whereby the contingent becomes essential', *The Future of Hegel*, 74.
17. There are plenty of seventeenth-century examples of this phrase. The popular *Aristotle's Master-Piece*, a work on human reproduction apocryphally attributed to Aristotle, states that the body's 'natural or vegetable soul' has a 'plastic power' which enables it to move and adopt various postures, whilst a 'plastic or formative principle' turns a lump of formless matter into a human shape in the womb, Anon, *Aristotle's Master-Piece*, trans. Anon (London: B. Harris, 1697), A4v, B4r. For several early modern natural philosophers, 'plastic power' was an unhelpfully vague and potentially fictitious idea that nobody could satisfactorily define; the Dutch physician Stephen Blankaart calls it 'a sure Refuge of Ignorance, for what the Ancients could not explain they called a plastick Virtue', *A Physical Dictionary* (London: J.D., 1684), Q5v.
18. Malabou, *The Future of Hegel*, 8. Sebastian Rand, translator of *What Should We Do with Our Brain?*, further evokes Renaissance culture by describing plasticity as 'self-fashioning', a phrase current in new historical Renaissance studies thanks to Stephen Greenblatt's *Renaissance Self-Fashioning: From More To Shakespeare* (Chicago: Chicago University Press, 1980); Malabou, *What Should We Do with Our Brain?*, 71.
19. Joseph Glanvill, *The Vanity of Dogmatizing* (London: E. C., 1661), E6r-v. In a later letter, Glanvill admits that he cannot tell whether these plastic faculties are a part of the body or the soul, 'whether, as your Grace inquires, they are Faculties inherent, in the Soul, or are only Mechanical Motions of the Body I cannot determine certainly', Joseph Glanvill, in various authors, *Letters and Poems in Honour of the Incomparable Princess, Margaret, Dutchess of Newcastle* (London: Thomas Newcombe, 1676), Dd2v, Ii2r-v.

20. Francis Bugg, *The Character of a Quaker* (London: SG, 1704) [broadside].
21. Mary Penington (daughter), *Mary Penington her Book, being copies of several Papers of friends, which she transcribed for her Dear Father*, M.S. Temp MSS 752, Friends Library and Archive, London [unsigned, unnumbered fols], 2r-v. Quaker Richard Moore wrote in 1662 to Quaker prisoners in Welshpool advising them to stay together as a Quaker group, sequester themselves in their cells, and kick up a fuss if they are not allowed to receive Quaker visitors, in order to stay steadfast in the Quaker faith, 'Dear Lambs the Lord is Weaning you from the world, therefore wait that your minds may be wholly gathered up unto him and especially let two hours be set apart every day to wait together, for the feeling of the Lords presence'. Figuring the imprisoned Quakers as young beings, 'Lambs' (and elsewhere 'Babes') still being weaned, Moore emphasises that their minds are in a newly-forming state (though, he promises, when ready God will 'bring you forth with your feet upon the necks of enemies, both within & without'), Letter from Richard Moore to Welshpool 4/12/1662, Item 23 in MS Vol 62, Friends Library and Archive, London, 25–6.
22. Ellwood, *The History*, C5r.
23. Ellwood, *The History*, F6r.
24. Cf. Michel Foucault, *Discipline and Punish*, trans. Alan Sheridan (London: Penguin, 1991), 138.
25. Malabou, *What Should We Do with Our Brain?*, 76; Malabou states that 'life' is 'resistance to flexibility (*What Should We Do with Our Brain?*, 68).
26. Malabou, *What Should We Do with Our Brain?*, 12.
27. Ellwood, *The History*, O7r-v.
28. Richard Haydock, *A Tracte Containing the Arts of Curious Painting, Carving and Building* (Oxford: for R. H., 1598), Aiiijr. The tract was first published in Italian in 1584; Haydock's translation (which he illustrated) is the first known treatise on painting published in English; Haydock translates 'plastica'.
29. Malabou, *What Should We Do with Our Brain?*, 7.
30. Malabou, *What Should We Do with Our Brain?*, 15.
31. Malabou, *What Should We Do with Our Brain?*, 15.
32. Nancy Jiwon Cho, 'Literature', *The Cambridge Companion to Quakerism* (69–87), 69.
33. Cho, 'Literature', 71–3.
34. Cho, 'Literature', 71–3.
35. Joseph Wyeth, 'Preface', in Ellwood, *The History*, a3v.
36. Nigel Smith, *Perfection Proclaimed: Language and Literature in English Radical Religion 1640–1660* (Oxford: Clarendon Press, 1989), 11.
37. Francis Bugg, *A Retrospective Glass for the Quakers* (London: Sold by R Wilkin, 1710), B1r.
38. Ellwood, *The History*, H3r-v; likewise, the Justice behaved 'courteously to *Isaac Penington*, as being a Gentleman of his *Neighbourhood*', Ellwood, *The History*, H2r. This is not the only time Thomas's class saves him; when Thomas is apprehended by the Watch, for example, a woman 'gave them such an account of my Father, as made them look more regardfully on me', H8r.
39. Smith, *Perfection Proclaimed*, 66–7. Mary Penington junior refers to this in

her commonplace book as 'the life and power of God planted in the heart and mind', *Mary Penington her Book*, 6r. As Rogers Healey explains, later, this tended towards complete elimination of the human will in the form of eighteenth-century Quietism, 'History of Quaker Faith and Practice', 25, 29.

40. Fox, *Journal*, 298.
41. Anon, *Some papers given forth to the world*, A4v-B1r.
42. Anon, *Some papers given forth to the world*, C4r-v.
43. Ellwood, *The History*, D5r.
44. Ellwood, *The History*, D6v.
45. Ellwood, *The History*, D4v.
46. Ellwood, *The History*, A1r-v.
47. Naomi Baker, '"Cross to my Honour": Status and Gender in the Life Writings of Mary Penington and Thomas Ellwood', *Quaker History* 91(1) (2002) (20–44), 20, 24.
48. Baker, '"Cross to my Honour"', 23–4, 34.
49. Baker, '"Cross to my Honour"', 35.
50. Ellwood, *The History*, C6r.
51. Ellwood, *The History*, G6r.
52. Ellwood, *The History*, C7r.
53. Ellwood, *The History*, C7r.
54. Ellwood, *The History*, D5r.
55. Ellwood, *The History*, Q6v.
56. Ellwood, *The History*, Q6v.
57. Ellwood, *The History*, Q7r.
58. Malabou, *Plasticity at the Dusk of Writing*, 36.
59. Bruce McConachie, *Theatre and Mind* (New York: Palgrave, 2013), 2–3.
60. Ellwood, *The History*, S7v.
61. Ellwood, *The History*, S3r.
62. Ellwood, *The History*, L3v.
63. Ellwood, *The History*, L4r.
64. Ellwood, *The History*, L4v.
65. Smith, *Perfection Proclaimed*, 9.

Chapter 4

Chaste and Silent – Again. Vitality and the Bound and Loosed Body in I. T.'s *Grim the Collier of Croydon; or, The Devil and His Dame* (c. 1600)

When we first meet her, as a marriageable young woman, it seems that Honorea has never spoken. Honorea's father Morgan, Earl of London, and his friend Lord Lacy of Kent read her silence as a sign of chastity and modesty, assuming that she would therefore make the perfect wife. In fact, as I explore in this chapter, Honorea's initial silence and outwardly docile behaviour barely conceal a simmering, subversive vitality, difficult to bind once set loose. Honorea is the central character in the probably-late-Elizabethan drama *Grim the Collier of Croydon; or, the Devil and his Dame*, attributed to 'I. T.', whose identity is uncertain. The plot centres around Morgan offering Honorea's hand in marriage to whichever man can make her speak; his plan is to marry her to the ageing Lacy. Honorea, however, is in love with a man called Musgrave, who reciprocates her love. A character called Castiliano enters, informing everyone that he is a Spanish doctor and promising to cure Honorea with a potion of magic herbs. Administering the potion, Castiliano loads the encounter with high expectations of hearing Honorea's 'Celestial voice', and though twice offering Honorea 'freedom' he caps it each time with the admonition that she will choose him as her husband. When Honorea does speak, it is with a torrent of abuse, angrily rejecting both Lacy and Castiliano, berating her father and thoroughly puncturing the men's expectation that her silence was the precursor to chaste, obedient speech:

> Castiliano: And by this juyce shall *Honorea* speak;
> Here Lady, drink the freedom of thy heart,
> And may it teach thee long to call me Love. [*She drinks*]
> Now lovely *Honorea* thou art free,
> Let thy Celestial voyce make choyce of me.
> Honorea: Base Alien, mercenary Fugitive,

>   Presumptuous Spaniard, that with shameless pride
>   Dar'st ask an English Lady for thy Wife.
>   I scorn, my slave should honour thee so much,
>   And for my self, I like myself the worse,
>   That thou dar'st hope the gaining of my Love.
>   Go, get thee gone, the shame of my esteem,
>   And seek some drudge that may be like thy self.
>   But as for you, good Earle of *Kent*,
>   Methinks your Lordship being of these years
>   Should be past dreaming of a second Wife.
>   Fy, fy, fy, my Lord 'ti[s] lust in doting age;
>   I will not patronise so foul a sin.
>   An old man dote on youth! 'tis monstrous;
>   Go home, go home, and rest your weary head,
>   'Twere pity such a brow should learn to bud.
>   And lastly, unto you, my Lord, and Father,
>   Your love to me is too much overseen
>   That in your care and counsell should devise
>   To tye your Daughter's choice to two such Grooms.
>   You may elect for me, but I'le dispose
>   And fit myself far better than both those.
>   And so I will conclude, you as you please.
>   [*Exit Honorea in a chafe*]
> Robin: Call you this making of a Woman speak?
>   I think they all wish she were dumb again.[1]

Honorea matches her volubility with angry bodily movement: she exits 'in a chafe' or temper.[2] Chafing was associated with vitality, physical heat, excitement, and aliveness; 'to chafe' could mean to heat the body and inflame the feelings (often in vexation).[3] Her outburst begins with crude xenophobia, classism, and ageism, and ends making a fair point: her father should not have chosen her a husband against her will. Robin Goodfellow bluntly signals the comedic import of the potion scene. His obvious remark attempts to contain what no doubt exceeded his neat couplet: Honorea's body brimming with rage, turning the tables on the male characters who had talked over her throughout the first three scenes of the play. This chapter explores the ways in which Honorea's bodily vitality ebbs and flows, exceeding and challenging the confines of the play's language. *Grim the Collier* is a fascinating example of how a character's vitality can knot speech and the body together, whilst also offering the potential for the body to assert its primacy over speech.

Honorea's fluctuating vitality is framed within the play's wider interest in ideals of docile female behaviour. As an earlier scene set in hell establishes, the self-assured doctor Castiliano is in fact the mild-natured devil Belphagor, who has come to earth in disguise to save women's reputations. Malbecco, the cuckold from Edmund Spenser's *The Faerie*

Queene III.ix-x (1590, 1596) has a cameo in *Grim the Collier*, arriving in hell to tell tales of women's adulterous lust.⁴ The infernal judges Minos, Aecus, Rhadamanth, and Pluto dispatch Belphagor and the demon Akercock (also known as Robin Goodfellow) to earth in human bodies to find out if the tales are true. The stakes are high because the infernal judges are deciding whether Malbecco killed himself (and thus will stay in hell) or was essentially killed by his wife Hellenore's terrible behaviour (and thus can potentially ascend to heaven as an innocent martyr). Belphagor does not fulfil his aim of demonstrating that women are sweet and lovable; his experience on earth proves quite the reverse.⁵ As we have seen, he gets Honorea to speak, but all she wants to do at first is insult everyone around her. He thereby wins Honorea's hand in marriage but is tricked into marrying her even more shrewish maid Marian instead. Terrified by these London women, Akercock flees the city to hide in the countryside until this disastrous holiday on earth is over. The tenth-century saint Dunstan (famous in earlier texts for grabbing the devil with a pair of tongs or tweaking the devil's nose when the devil tried to distract him from playing a harp) manages to bind Honorea's tongue again and tie her in marriage to Lacy. Belphagor, however, is not so lucky as Lacy. Marian has extramarital affairs and finally attempts to murder Belphagor. By the end of the play, cuckolded, poisoned, and robbed, Belphagor is only too glad to get home to hell. Encircled by humans keen to do them harm, Belphagor and Akercock shoot gratefully downwards through the stage trapdoor, their abrupt exit having a comedic effect:

> Belphagor: Lordings adieu, and my curst Wife farewell,
> If me ye seek, come follow me to Hell. [*The Ground opens, and he falls down into it*]
> Morgan: The Earth that opened, now is clos'd again!⁶

Grim the Collier, then, has the structure of a joke. The punchline? Women's shrewishness makes earth worse than hell.

Within this play-length joke, the loosing and binding of Honorea both challenges conventional Christian notions of desirable female behaviour and involves a poignant personal tragedy for Honorea herself as she is ultimately 'bound' to a suitor she had never previously loved. *Grim the Collier* invokes Christian ideals of the silent and obedient woman, stemming particularly from 1 Timothy 2:11–12 ('Let the woman learn in silence with all subjection. I permit not a woman to teach, neither to usurp authority over the man, but to be in silence') and 1 Corinthians 14:34–35 ('Let your women keep silence in the Churches: for it is not permitted unto them to speak: but they ought to be subject, as also the

Law saith ... it is a shame for women to speak in the Church').[7] In c. 1600, when *Grim* was probably written and performed, these ideas had been in existence for several centuries and would remain current for several more; in 1629, clergyman Thomas Adams wrote that a wife ought to cultivate a 'still and mild' manner to demonstrate her recognition that her husband was 'her better', 'favouring all quietness and lowliness of affection ... her reverence doth enjoin her silence when she stands by'.[8] Characters in *Grim* repeatedly hold these conventions bathetically up to reality. This occurs from the early scenes when Akercock punctures Belphagor's high expectations for his trip:

Belphagor: In lovely *London* are we here arrived,
Whereas I hear the Earl hath a fair Daughter
So full of vertue and soft modesty
That yet she never gave a man foul word
Akercock: Marry indeed, they say she cannot speak.[9]

Akercock reminds Belphagor that Honorea 'never gave a man foul word' not necessarily because of any innate 'vertue and soft modesty' but rather because she simply 'cannot speak'. The play cannot be reduced to such jokes, however. Rather, *Grim*'s treatment of Honorea's vitality – curbed, then unrestrained, then curbed again – draws richly on folkloric and biblical narratives and Reformation beliefs about exorcism and the powers of God's representatives on earth. Ultimately, the ways in which the peaks and troughs in characters' bodily energy can kinesically engage the audience's own bodies are more compelling than Akercock's throwaway lines.

In exploring women's (non-)ideal behaviour through the trope of an unhappy marriage between a shrew and a devil, I. T. follows an early modern tradition. As Robert Shuler explains, the trope of the voluble shrew as the devil's dam was common in sixteenth- and early seventeenth-century drama; worse than the devil, the shrew makes hell preferable to married life.[10] Plays and jest-book tales about shrews and devils stem from folkloric material predating the Renaissance; a key fifteenth-century folkloric source is the Friar Rush myth (which I examined in Chapter 1) of a devil disguised as a man, infiltrating human society and responding with delight and occasionally shock to humans' talent for wickedness. In Ben Jonson's *The Devil Is an Ass* (1616) the devil Pug is naïve compared to scheming humans; like Belphagor he 'wish[es]l To be in hell againe, at leasure'.[11] John Heywood's *The Foure PP* (1544) evokes shrewish women in hell tormenting the devils so much 'that all the deuyls be wery of theyr lyfe'.[12] Until around 1500, 'shrew' was a synonym for the devil; throughout the seventeenth century 'shrew' and devil were both epicoene words that could refer to someone of any gender.[13] This enabled comparisons between devils and shrews and a blurring of identities befitting their often intimate relationship whether as a married pair or because the devil has possessed the shrew.

Grim falls within a specific strand of shrew-devil literature focusing on the tender-hearted devil Belphagor who takes on human flesh and all its frailties and is roundly abused by his shrewish wife and her associates. Niccolò Machiavelli's 1515–20 novella *Belfagor Arcidiavolo* is an obvious source for *Grim*. Machiavelli's Belfagor is a model husband, financially and emotionally abused by his shrewish wife Onesta and her family.[14] *Grim*'s Belphagor is 'patient, mild and pittifull' before leaving Hell, making him more of a poor victim perhaps than Machiavelli's Belfagor who acquires the human 'weaknesses' of mild-manners and law-abidingness only upon assuming human form.[15] Sante Matteo argues that Machiavelli's attractively compassionate and just devils critique the injustice and violence of earthly societies.[16] Barnabe Riche's relatively honest, loving, and decent devil in *Riche's Farewell to The Military Profession* (1583), though he is renamed Balthaser, is influenced both by Machiavelli and by Giovanni Francesco Straparola's version in *Le Piacevoli Notti* (1557). Tormented by his wife Mildred's constant demand for new clothes, Balthaser provides the familiar punchline: 'I had rather be in hell, than maried to suche a wife'.[17]

Though it can clearly be placed within this tradition, *Grim the Collier* is a rather mysterious play. It was first published, over 60 years after its projected first performance, in *Gratiae Theatrales*: a 1662 anthology of four plays. The author may have been William Haughton (d. 1605) who wrote several plays for Henslowe's Admiral's men and appears in Henslowe's diary as receiving a loan 'in earneste of a boocke wch he wold calle the devell & his dame' (i.e., *Grim*'s alternative title); Henslowe crossed out the entry, perhaps to indicate that the money was returned as the book was not provided.[18] Another less likely candidate, suggested by the authorial initials 'I. T.' in *Gratiae Theatrales*, is John Tatham (fl. 1632–64).[19] I refer to the author of *Grim* as 'I. T.', a placeholder for a murky authorship debate. After *Gratiae Theatrales*, *Grim* was patchily performed and anthologised, with editions appearing once or twice a century.[20] The eponymous Grim the Collier, who appears in *Grim*'s comic subplot as one of the rustic people Akercock escapes to live among, was a stock comic character appearing from the late sixteenth to mid-seventeenth century in a variety of plays and prose pamphlets.[21]

Grim stands out from these various theatrical and literary traditions in the revealing way I. T. stages bodily vitality through pervasive language of binding and loosing: from Honorea's bound and loosed tongue to Dunstan's bound and loosed harp strings, to the bonds between characters (Morgan says that Honorea's shrewishness serves only to 'bind' him to Lacy more, for instance), to the finale where Honorea is 'tyed' in marriage with Lacy, whose very name suggest strings, laces, and tying.[22] Dunstan is an almost ubiquitous presence in *Grim*; in the potion scene, Belphagor grapples with Dunstan over who can 'cure' Honorea quickest. Morgan and Lacy want Dunstan to 'loose' Honorea's tongue so that she can verbally consent to marry Lacy. In fact, only Belphagor/Castiliano manages to loose her tongue, with his potion. In post-Reformation England binding and loosing referred to priests' disputed powers to remit sins, and (relatedly) to God's representatives' power to exorcise demons; these senses derived from the Bible. Jesus tells Peter, 'I will give unto thee the keys of the Kingdom of heaven, and whatsoever thou shalt bind upon earth, shall be bound in heaven: and whatsoever thou shalt loose on earth, shall be loosed in heaven' (Matthew 16:19). He then offers this power to all his disciples, 'Verily I say unto you, whatsoever ye bind on earth, shall be bound in heaven: and whatsoever ye loose on earth, shall be loosed in heaven' (Matthew 18:18). This power to bind and loose came to be known in the Christian church as 'the power of the keys'. As Ronald Rittgers explains, early modern Catholics took it to endorse the sacrament of penance through confession; Lutherans challenged this traditional power, though they still 'took Christ's giving of the keys to Peter as proof that God intended for the Church to bind and loose sins'.[23] While Lutherans created 'a new evangelical version of the keys' (private confession that was not sacramental, and less detailed than traditional sacramental confession, and confession in groups rather than one-on-one with the priest), Rittgers writes, Reformed Protestants like Calvinists rejected it outright.[24] In Reformed England, the power of ministers like Dunstan (who was an Abbot and Bishop) to bind and loose sins and demons on earth was open to mockery as an officially-rejected Catholic belief. Nevertheless, the idea retained power, lingering in Elizabethan Protestant culture as what (as we saw in Chapter 1) Woods calls an 'unreformed fiction': a representation of Catholic beliefs, practices, and people in a fictional space that does not necessarily represent contemporary Catholic doctrine.[25]

Tracing Catholic and Protestant debates over the power of the keys, Richard Hiers highlights the pervasive use of terminology of binding and loosing to refer to people being both exorcised and 'cured' of ailments – often indicating both at once. The devil or ailment 'binds' a person and God's representative 'looses' the afflicted person, often by 'binding' any devil involved. Hiers explains, in intertestamental writings and in the N[ew] T[estament], the terms "binding" and "loosing" are commonly used in connection with the overcoming of Satan and/or the demons and the freeing of their victims, either in the past or at the judgment that is to come or during the remainder of the present age. In these various contexts those doing the binding and loosing include the holy angels (or archangels) of God, the coming messiah or priest, Jesus, and certain other exorcists.[26]

Exorcism is a key aspect of the Belphagor myth; Machiavelli's Belfagor possesses various wealthy women, allowing a peasant he is in cahoots with to 'exorcise' them for profit. In *Grim the Collier*, Belphagor performs a kind of 'exorcism' or 'cure' of Honorea that is also an attempt to take possession of her (as his wife). Thereby, he sets Honorea's tongue and behaviour 'loose' in a way he and the other characters quickly find undesirable, leading Dunstan to 'bind' her tongue again and 'tye' her in marriage to Lacy, with Morgan and Lacy's approval.

Grim's vocabulary of binding and loosing rests on a range of New Testament biblical precedents relating to exorcism and 'cure'. In Revelations 20:1–2 an angel using a chain and a key 'bound' Satan in the bottomless pit for a thousand years, with the foreboding fear that later 'Satan shall be loosed out of his prison'. In Mark 5:2–4, a possessed man could, as a mark of his possession, not be bound:

> And when he was come out of the ship, there met him incontinently out of the graves, a man which had an unclean spirit: Who had his abiding among the graves, and no man could bind him, no not with chains: Because that when he was often bound with fetters and chains, he plucked the chains asunder, and brake the fetters in pieces, neither could any man tame him.

Mark 7:34–35 describes a deaf and non-verbal man 'loosed' by Jesus so that he begins to speak and hear. Hiers points out, 'here, as in several other places ... a healing or "miracle" story bears traces of an exorcism narrative', linked by common vocabulary of binding and loosing: the man's tongue is 'loosed' in contrast to devils and demoniacs alike who are 'tied shut/silenced'.[27] Early modern authors often describe non-verbal people (popularly, King Croesus' son or Justinian's captain Battas) having their tongues 'tied' by their disability and 'loosed' when cured.[28] In Mark 3:27, Jesus uses a metaphor of a strong man who is bound, to describe exorcism, 'No man can enter into a strong man's house, and take away his goods, except he first bind that strong man, and then spoil his house'. This metaphor is open to several readings. If Satan is the strong man, the exorcist the person who spoils his house, and the house the possessed person's body, to bind the strong man and rob and spoil his house is a positive act. Alternatively the possessed person may be the strong man, bound by Satan, who then ransacks his house (i.e., his soul, body, and mind). *Grim* stages this potential ambiguity by representing Honorea's 'cure' as unwanted. In loosing Honorea, Belphagor endows her with hallmarks of demonic possession – being bound by the devil – until she is (re)possessed and bound more acceptably by God and the patriarchy working through Dunstan. Indeed, as I showed in Chapter 1, devils often entered into their victims through unblessed food and drink; Belphagor's potion seems a (spiritually) poisoned chalice. I. T. thereby taps in to popular contemporary depictions of the false or staged 'cure' I examined in Chapter 2.

Dunstan asserts his ability to 'cure' Honorea with recognisably Catholic practices and sacred objects: fasting, 'religious works', a mass, 'three sips of the holy Challice', prayers on the rosary, aves, and creeds. *Grim* also stages the mockery of such rites:

> Dunstan: . . . your daughter must be cur'd
> By fasting prayer, and religious works;
> My self for her will sing a solemn mass,
> And give her three sips of the holy Challice,
> And turn my Beads with Aves and with Creeds,
> And thus, my *Lord*, your Daughter must be help'd.
> Castiliano Zowndes, what a prating keeps the bald-pate Fryer?
> My Lord, my Lord, here's Church work for an age!
> Tush, I will cure her in a minutes space[29]

Dunstan's inability either to 'cure' Honorea or (as we shall see) to 'loose' the strings of his own harp suggests that he does not have St Peter's power to bind and loose. However the fact that the person who does cure Honorea is Belphagor, a devil, calls into question the desirability of such a power. Indeed, the patriarchal preference Lacy voices early in the play for a 'bound', controlled Honorea is ultimately validated by most of the men around her, 'In vain it is for us to think to loose/ That which by Natures self we see is bound'.[30] Lacy thereby articulates both the patriarchy's desire for power and a reformed critique of Dunstan's unreformed pretensions.

Belphagor's potion can be read as both binding and loosing Honorea, insofar as her loosed tongue may signal that she is bound to the devil by drinking his potion. By drinking, she is legibly both exorcised of her speechlessness and possessed by a wicked-speaking devil. I examine these issues through the lens of vitality, tracking the compelling ebb and flow of Honorea's bodily energy. Her vitality surges forth after drinking the potion, then Dunstan curbs and weakens it again. At key points, *Grim* invites us to read Honorea's thoughts and emotions kinesically in ways that contradict her and other characters' descriptions of what she is thinking and feeling. For example, at the (to most other characters) supposedly happy ending when Honorea and Lacy's marriage is confirmed, Honorea's body belies the 'joy' she diplomatically claims to feel by collapsing to the ground as if seeking the blessed escape of death: '*She falleth into a Sound*'.³¹

Honorea's fluctuating vitality echoes and interacts with the ebbs and flows of other characters' vitality: Kent sickens and revives, for example, the latter event prompting Honorea, contrastingly, to fall into her swoon, and Dunstan sleeps then awakes to 'lay[sic] about him with his staff'. Dunstan seems to tire himself out with delivering the play's opening monologue; overwhelmed by sleepiness, his ebbing vitality is matched by a corresponding surge in the devils' liveliness as they plot to invade earth. The devils' activity is countered in its turn by a revival of Dunstan's vitality as he springs back up. The overall effect prompts us to engage kinetically and kinaesthetically with the action on stage and page.

> Dunstan: But on a sudden I'm o'ercome with sleep!
> If ought ensue, watch you, for *Dunstan* dreams
> [*He layeth him down to sleep. The curtain drawn to reveal devils*].³²

The devils' plot laid, Dunstan springs into bounding motion, '*Dunstan rising, runneth about the stage, laying about him with his staff*', shouting 'Sathan avaunt'.³³ The contrast between Dunstan's languorous sleep and the vigorously-plotting devils, and between Dunstan's sleep and his later acceleration as he 'runneth' and attacks the devils, can immediately engage audiences' kinesic responses. Dunstan asks us to 'watch', and without any need for us to pause and evaluate what is happening, the performer playing Dunstan communicates the force and withdrawal of their vitality to us. When the saint reduces himself to a stiller, fainter presence on stage, the devils gain power. When Dunstan springs back up to chase the devils his surging vitality mingles with the devils', offering audiences a correspondingly energising feeling of release that does not necessarily differentiate between saint and devil. Living through the timespan of this cresting, then diminishing, then cresting again offers us a bodily release we may find comic: it is hilarious when a sleeper springs up and starts running furiously about. Nevertheless, attention to the text remains important in understanding the complex possible significations of these movements. By re-using the verb-form 'lay-' with two different suffixes ('layeth', 'laying') to describe Dunstan lying down horizontally to sleep and swinging his staff around to attack the devils, I. T. emphasises the link between surging and curbed vitality, situating them both in the same textual character and performing body. Making Dunstan's body the intriguing source of both force and weakness is on one level a theatrical strategy: as audiences we are compelled to keep watching as we wonder (and the play asks us to wonder as Belphagor tests Dunstan's 'force') which he will demonstrate next.

The psychologist Daniel Stern formulated the idea of vitality in the 1980s, tracing the idea's history to nineteenth-century vitalism, and affirming a neurological basis to vitality in neural arousal. Stern argues that vitality is a kinetic life-force, energy or excitement in and of itself, 'the domain of dynamic forms of vitality is separate and distinct from the domains of emotion, sensation, and cognition'.[34] Like Sheets-Johnstone, Stern affirms the primacy of bodily movement in expressions of (mental) life; for Stern, 'vitality forms are not readily describable in words', indeed describing vitality saps its power.[35] Central to how we engage with others, vitality ebbs and flows and is marked by intentionality. Stern analyses vitality as key to 'time-based arts' such as theatre; such arts, he argues, cause peaks and troughs in the audience's 'arousal level' as well as perhaps the performer and writer's.[36] Examining alternations between surging movement and stillness in games and theatre (specifically in *The Winter's Tale*), Hannah Chapelle Wojciehowski asserts that onlookers can feel 'an onrush of vitality' transferred from actors' or game-players' bodies to ours.[37] Raphael Lyne explains the value of attending to vitality in early modern performance,

> kinesic intelligence needs to, because it can, reach beyond gestures, responses, and intentions, into the fainter fundamentals of life, things which are always with us but rarely perceived, signs that may be most accessible, and most strangely accessible, when we think through what it would take to perform them.[38]

This chapter 'think[s] through what it would take to perform' Honorea's fluctuating vitality, and the ways this relates to early modern misogyny and (un)reformed religion. As Stern, Wojciehowski and Lyne all emphasise, vitality plays out over time, fluctuating in terms of its force, intentionality, and directionality.[39] *Grim the Collier*'s vocabulary gives clues about all these features of Honorea's vitality, as other characters comment on the forms her vitality takes, but cannot quite capture these vitality forms in language.

Grim is populated with vocabulary of vitality: as we have seen, the play involves characters swooning, fainting, sleeping, laying about with a staff, running, being tied, bound, loosed, tamed, and chafing; all evocative vitality forms. Stern offers a list of words relating to vitality, including:

> exploding, swelling, drawn out, forceful, cresting, rushing, relaxing, fluttering, tense, gliding, holding still, surging, bursting, disappearing, powerful,

Chaste and Silent – Again. 91

pulsing, pulling, languorous, effortful, gentle, swinging, loosely, accelerating, fading, fleeting, weak, tentative, pushing, floating, easy, halting, tightly, [and] bounding.[40]

Stern explains of his list,

> The items in it are not emotions. They are not motivational states. They are not pure perceptions. They are not sensations in the strict sense, as they have no modality. They are not direct cognitions in any usual sense. They are not acts, as they have no goal state and no specific means. They fall in between all the cracks. They are the felt experience of force – in movement – with a temporal contour, and a sense of aliveness, of going somewhere. They do not belong to any particular content. They are more form than content. They concern the "How," the manner, and the style, not the "What" or the "Why."'[41]

Though, as we have seen, we might interpret binding and loosing within Biblical and misogynist frameworks, Stern's arguments illuminate the ways in which these terms are also forms of vitality: irreducible states of kinetic being. Examining the 'how' in this performance – how Honorea surges forth, then falters and faints – illuminates the play's compelling effect.

Once Honorea has jilted Castiliano, Castiliano relates that when he went to offer Lacy 'counsel' about his wife, Lacy 'turns me up his Whites, and falls flat down;| There I was fain to rub and chafe his veins,| And much ado we had to get him live'.[42] The contrast between Castiliano's rubbing and chafing and Kent's complete lack of movement is another example of the ways in which in this play a single body, or contact between bodies, is a site of surging vitality and ebbing vitality all at once. It is unclear why Castiliano made this visit; indeed, whether deliberately or not, the devil clearly did more harm than good here, as Lacy next enters displaying an enervation so total he nears death. Dunstan enters 'with Earle Lacy sicke' and Lacy's dimming vitality is highlighted with four words here suggesting debility (sickness, feebleness, weakened, age): 'Let not your sickness adde more feebleness| Unto your weakened age . . .'[43] The potion scene contains a similar combination of surging and curbing vitality as Honorea silences the men around her with her rageful voice.

Nominally, Honorea is ultimately 'tamed' by St Dunstan, who renders her body weak, and her language clipped and obedient. As with her angry outburst in Act I, Honorea's voice in Act IV is again set up as a response or punchline to a male character's express expectations. Whilst in Act I, Honorea comedically defied Belphagor's expectation that she would speak in a 'Celestial Voice' obedient to his desires, in Act IV, Honorea speaks exactly as Dunstan asks. Paralleling Belphagor's thwarted promise of a 'Celestial Voice', Dunstan promises his fellow male characters 'vertuous chast replies' and Honorea delivers them, describing her heart 'tyed' to the ideal mode of life the patriarchy wants for her, and tying her words together in a rhyming couplet:

> Dunstan: Here comes the unstained honor of thy Bed,
> Thy Eares shall hear her vertuous chast replies,
> And make thy heart confess thou dost her wrong.
> Honorea: Now modest love hath banished wanton thoughts,
> And altered me from what I was before:
> To that chaste life I ought to entertain,
> My heart is tyed to that strick't form of life,
> That I joy only to be *Lacy's* wife . . .[44]

Honorea's heart and tongue are safely 'tyed', no longer expressing what she a few lines later calls 'loose desires'. Dunstan ostensibly triumphs at the end of *Grim the Collier*, displaying a simultaneously tamed and verbal Honorea just as Morgan and Lacy desired. Honorea's body tells a different story in this final scene: fainting and weeping when she hears Lacy (whom everyone had thought was on the brink of death) is still alive and still keen to marry her. When we first meet Honorea, though Morgan and Lacy take advantage of her silence and talk over her, her silence does not indicate a lack of sexual autonomy and desire, nor does it render her weak. She is a potent presence with a social network of her own; before the play's action begins Honorea has acquired a lover – Musgrave – and developed a strong friendship with Marian. Musgrave remains in love with Honorea throughout the play, and Marian is willing to participate in a bed-trick, marrying a devil, for Honorea's sake. Honorea's vitality often exists in contradistinction to the patriarchal assumptions that Dunstan, Morgan, and Lacy make about who she is and what she wants.

Tyed Tongues

Describing Honorea, the male characters rely on early modern ideas of tongue-strings bound and loosed to curb and unleash speech.[45] These ideas informed representations of possessed people speaking in tongues, or having their tongues tied by a devil so they could not speak (as in Mark 7:34–35). I. T. thereby implicates Honorea's ability to speak in a power-play between the male characters. This reflects the broader ways in which early modern authors implicated women's tongue-strings in (anti-)feminist debates.

Before Belphagor 'unbinds' Honorea's tongue, he and Dunstan compete over who can bind and loose Dunstan's harp strings. Gloatingly,

Belphagor binds the harp strings so that Dunstan cannot play his own harp. To further showcase his demonic power and Dunstan's inefficacy, Belphagor makes the harp play itself as it hangs on the wall. This devilish miracle was perhaps effected by hanging the harp in front of a curtain enabling a performer to reach their hand through a slit in the curtain and play the harp.[46] Dunstan and Belphagor's tussle over the harp foreshadows their tussle over Honorea and frames Honorea as primarily a tied-up instrument to be loosed and played upon by other people. It is no coincidence that the harp starts to play right after Belphagor proclaims, 'she shall speak as plain as you or I': Belphagor makes Honorea and the harp interchangeable, equating his power over both.[47] Dunstan attempts to save face by arguing that an angel is invisibly playing the harp 'to testify Dunstan's integrity', however Belphagor's statement that he has wrested control of the harp from Dunstan – 'the harp hath got another master now' – is borne out by the stage direction '*He [Dunstan] tryes to play, but cannot*'.[48] Dunstan then accuses Belphagor, 'by thy spells dost hold these holy strings'; Belphagor taunts him, 'Cannot your Holyness unbind the bonds? Then I perceive my skill is most of force', again prefiguring his unbinding of Honorea's tongue with his herbs that 'bind and unbind Nature's strongest powers'.[49] This connects Honorea's newfound ability to speak with Belphagor's (rather than Honorea's) superior 'force'. As we shall see later, her shrewish tongue indeed seems a separate entity, divorced from her own volition, and to be grappled with by the men around her. Initially hell's power triumphs over harp and tongue; ultimately, however, Dunstan demonstrates a god-given ability to 'bind' on earth. When asked to cure Honorea, Dunstan states that only God can 'bind' and 'loose' speech: 'the hallow'd gift of tongues| Comes from the selfsame power that gives us breath.| He binds and looseth them at his dispose'.[50] Dunstan suggests that not he himself, but God working through him, enables him to bind and loose Honorea.

The ultimate aim of all this binding and unbinding is not really to free Honorea but rather to demonstrate and rank the male characters' power. Despite Morgan's insistence that he wants his daughter 'cured', the male characters clearly prefer Honorea bound to Honorea loose.[51] Lacy pays lip service to the idea that it would be wonderful to hear Honorea speak, but his repetition of 'bound' links her silence to agreeably mild and undisruptive behaviour. Addressing Morgan, Lacy attests,

> My Lord of *London*, now long time it is
> Since Lacy first was suiter to your Daughter,
> The fairest *Honorea*, in whose eyes
> Honor it self in Love's sweet bosom lyes:
> What shall we say, or seem to strive with heaven,

> Who speechless sent her first into the world;
> In vain it is for us to think to loose
> That which by Natures self we see is bound:
> Her beauty, with her other vertues joyn'd,
> Are gifts sufficient, though she want a tongue;
> And some will count it Vertue in a woman
> Still to be bound to un-offending Silence;
> Though I could wish with half of all my Lands,
> That she could speak: but since it may not be,
> 'Twere vain to impose on Beauty with her speech . . .[52]

Honorea is tied up like a parcel: her tongue, virtues, and physical attractiveness 'join'd' together for Lacy's taking. Her tongue is not just physically 'bound' and thus silent: Honorea is also 'bound' to the concept of 'unoffending silence' itself. Lacy discourages earthly people from attempting to loose what seems naturally bound, arguing that it would be futile to try. *Grim* comically invokes (post-)Reformation debates about whether people have such power, and whether it comes from God or the devil. I. T. uses Honorea's rampaging tongue to make a theological point about God's superior power over the devil as Belphagor admits he is only able to loose Honorea's tongue, not bind it, simultaneously conjuring a bathetic image of Dunstan wrangling with Honorea's tongue with his rosary:

> Lacy: I would to God her Tongue were tyed again.
> Castiliano: I marry Sir, but that's an other thing.
>   The Devil cannot tye a Woman's tongue,
>   I would the Fryer could do that with his Beads[53]

On one level, to tie Honorea's tongue with beads could simply be metaphorical, meaning that Dunstan will silence Honorea through the power of his prayers, as Dunstan himself has suggested. However, exemplifying the strong physicality of *Grim*'s binding imagery throughout the play, Castiliano on another level represents Dunstan grappling with Honorea's tongue, attempting to wrest it into submission by wrapping his rosary around it. Indeed, given the Spenserian influence evident in *Grim* with Malbecco's cameo early on, I. T. may also have been influenced, in the depiction of Dunstan confronting furious Honorea, by Spenser's description of Guyon and the hag Occasion. Guyon 'with an yron locke did fasten firme and strong' the tongue of Occasion so that he could then tie her hands and bind her son Furor in a variety of knots and chains; Furor strains against these bonds, his passionate desire for violent revenge contrasting with the largely stock-still position Guyon has enforced on him.[54] Spenser uses vitality-filled imagery of a river 'stopped' (damned-up) and breaking its banks to describe

Furor and Occasion's destructively free-flowing rancour.[55] Like Guyon silencing Occasion by placing a lock on her tongue, Dunstan tying Honorea's tongue with his rosary invites the reader creatively to exercise their imagination. Castiliano's image might suggest a number of bodily interactions, from Honorea having a large flapping tongue long enough for Dunstan to lasso with his rosary to Dunstan craning into Honorea's mouth attempting to noose her slippery, wriggling tongue with his beads. No matter the precise interaction we kinesically imagine, Castiliano's description positions Dunstan and Honorea in a ridiculous imagined posture and reduces Dunstan's binding to an ineffective physical wrestle with Honorea's tongue.

Grim is part of a broader use of imagery of binding and loosing in early modern discourses of volubility, constraint, and gendered agency. Early feminist writer Jane Anger, in her extraordinary *Her Protection for Women* (1589) subverts contemporary assumptions that volubility is an unsavoury female trait. I adduce Anger because her text demonstrates the ways in which notions of binding and loosing could develop their original biblical context in richly gendered and polemical ways. Anger argues that in fact it is men who talk too much, using their privilege to wield language damagingly against women:

> FIE on the falshoode of men, whose minds goe oft a madding, & whose tongues cannot so soone bee wagging, but straight they fal a railing. Was there ever any so abused, so slaundered, so railed upon, or so wickedly handeled undeservedly, as are we women?[56]

Anger's homoioteleuton in the first sentence, and prolixity throughout the passage quoted above, performs even as it chastises the loose 'wagging' tongue. Anger argues that men's excessive use of the written word is paradoxically too wicked to put into words, describing it as 'unspeakable'. She adds that this leads men's speech to become 'carried away' beyond what they themselves can understand: 'often times they overrun the boundes of their own wits'.[57]

For Anger, strings facilitate oral and written language (the strings of the tongue and fingers, the brain's stretching veins, and the vocal chords) but stringy restraints can also limit expression. In her preliminary address stretching out 'To all Women in generall', Anger calls for 'a halter' to 'hold' women's enemies. In a sentence extending itself clause by clause like the stretching bodily and mental attributes she describes, she states, 'Shal Surfeiters raile on our kindnes, you stand stil & say nought, and shall not Anger stretch the vaines of her braines, the stringes of her fingers, and the listes of her modestie, to answere their Surfeitings'.[58] In 1589, 'lists' could mean 'desires', earlobes, the sense of hearing or attention, the boundary of a territory, any strip of cloth (often, the OED's examples suggest, used for tying bundles or clothing together), and specifically a strip of cloth hemming or bordering a garment or piece of fabric. Its etymology, from the Old French *liste* ('weak, feminine'), suggests a strong link between gendered weakness and the state of being restrained. Anger seems to put all of these meanings into play: displaying a lack of 'feminine weakness' and ignoring the boundaries others would impose on her abilities, understanding, and behaviour, Anger's desires shoot forth to attack misogynists, her ears lengthen to catch their wicked speech, and she attends to their 'Surfeitings' despite it requiring immodest attention. Her modest attire or behaviour stretches to or beyond its limit; or in a feminine image of embroidery (which would fit her next paragraph's discussion of men wanting 'to smell at our smockes' and 'catch at our petticoats') the cloth she works with and wears, and which men snatch at, shoots forth to bind and tie her detractors. She calls later in the pamphlet for bonds to tie and 'bridle' men's tongues, bodies, and behaviour ('if wee doe desire to have them good, we must alwaies tie them to the manger and diet their greedy panches') and calls for 'every man ... to strive to bridle his slanderous tongue'.[59] As if enacting this 'bridling', the misogynistic text Anger is responding to, her printer Thomas Orwin's 'His Surfeit in Love', though entered in the Stationers' Register, is now lost (if it was ever printed). The only source material we now have for this text are the passages Anger deigns to quote as a springboard for her critique.

Grim was probably written in the wake of Anger's polemic, around a decade later. In *Grim*, as in *Her Protection for Women*, women's loosened bodily strings are sites of power, danger, and retribution. Other early modern texts – notably George Chapman's *The Widow's Tears* (c. 1609) which features diatribes against women's loose tongues – link loose tongues to women's sexually 'loose' behaviour, hypocrisy, drunkenness, mendacity, and inability to keep their resolve.[60] In a visceral image Anger suggests that, in contrast to her own stretchy body, men feel confident because their tongues do not extend so far as to put them in danger of grasping female fingers which could pull them out as a punishment: 'their slaunderous tongues are so short ... they know we cannot catch hold of them to pull them out'.[61] Kinesically, Anger's image reverses Castiliano's suggestion that Dunstan tie Honorea's tongue with his beads: Anger represents vengeful women grappling ridiculously with men's tongues. Simultaneously, Anger suggests as Castiliano does in his image of the beads, that women have especially long tongues. Both Anger and the author of *Grim* position language as a bodily battle between binary genders: men and women seek to extend their bodies' strings whilst restraining each other's bodies. In *Grim*, the threat of the onrush of vitality manifested in Honorea's devilishly loosened tongue strings and bodily tendons is countered by a gendered desire 'to bridle [her] slanderous tongue'. In the comic sub-plot, Grim describes his love for Joan as a painful ligature in his heart, a halter constraining him, 'methinks I have a Taylor sowing stitches in my Heart . . . I am so haltered in affection'.[62]

Grim attributes loosened mouths to all three of the women characters: Honorea, Marian, and Marian's maid Nan. Belphagor attempts to stop all of these mouths. Whilst Marian is busy conducting an adulterous affair at home, her husband 'Castiliano' returns unexpectedly. Marian's servant, Nan, cries out to warn her:

Nan:	Alas my Master is come home himself:
	Mistriss Mistriss, my Master is come home,
	[*he stops her mouth*]
Castiliano:	Peace you young Strumpet, or I'le stop your speech[63]

Curiously, in the original *Gratiae Theatrales*, Castiliano's threat to 'stop [Nan's] speech' comes after the stage direction, '*he stops her mouth*.' This may simply be a printer's error. Nevertheless it raises some of the play's central questions about characters' power over their own and others' speech and behaviour. On one reading, if the stage direction is correctly placed, Castiliano's own speech is ironically somewhat redundant as he has already 'stopped' Nan's mouth when he threatens 'or I'le stop your speech'. He fears Nan's speech's power to damage his life, yet his own redundant speech just adds to the noise he wants to prevent. He contributes to the kerfuffle that alerts Marian to his early return. Another reading is possible if 'stop your speech' refers not to the act of 'he stops her mouth' but rather promises further, even murderous, stopping. At any rate, Castiliano swiftly destabilises his threat when he subsequently relies on Nan's 'speech' to inform him what is going on. 'Tell me, and tell me true, what means this banquet' he asks, referring to the romantic supper Marian is preparing to enjoy in his absence:

Nan:	Forsooth I cannot tell.
Castiliano:	Can you not tell: come on, I'le make you tell me.
Nan:	O Master! I will tell you.[64]

Nan's 'I cannot tell' refers to the external agencies stopping her tongue – loyalty to Marian and fear of losing her job – as well, perhaps, to her own modesty. Colloquially, too, 'I cannot tell' could mean 'I don't know', so Nan is perhaps also feigning ignorance here.

The mismatch between language and body when, having already stopped Nan's mouth, Castiliano threatens to 'stop [her] speech', exemplifies the ways in which vitality exceeds language in this play. Paying attention to Honorea's tongue as 'stringy' fruitfully implicates it in ideas of vitality: the vibrating harp foreshadows the stretching, flapping tongue which must be physically wrestled with, in an act of exorcism that seems more like a blundering attempt to muzzle an unwieldy serpent.

Vitality and Autonomy

Just because a shrew is a vital (voluble, physically imposing, highly kinetic) presence on stage, does not mean that this vitality indicates her autonomous agency, self-possession, or true freedom. When, in Shakespeare's *The Taming of the Shrew* (c. 1590), Katherine bursts on stage hauling the Widow and Bianca about, her display of physical vigour is an obedient response to Petruchio's request to 'swinge me them soundly forth unto their husbands' (5.2.104). *Grim* decouples Honorea's surging vitality from her autonomy; however, just as her outburst into angry speech and movement does not necessarily signal that she has gained power and autonomy, Honorea's weakened, laconic final appearance does not necessarily signal that she is happily tamed. If, as Wojciehowski's work suggests, an audience's immediate kinesic response to Honorea's bodily vitality is one of delight and a sympathetic upsurge in our own vitality, this can be very much at odds with the more disturbing and complex dynamics which unfold when we take the time to think consciously about Honorea. Indeed, our delighted bodily responses can make us complicit in the play's patriarchal framework and the devil's show of power.

When Honorea bursts into speech and unruly motion, she can be read both as asserting her own will and as someone bound to the devil. These two readings are not contradictions; many early modern Christians would agree that a woman, Eve, exercising her flawed power to choose is what plunged humanity into original sin. As Morgan states, 'young Girles must have their Wills restrain'd'.[65] Honorea's (to Belphagor, Lacy, and Morgan) undesirable vitality centres around her loosened tongue. Tormented after Honorea first breaks into speech, Belphagor describes Honorea's tongue as 'like a Scarecrow in a tree'.[66] Consonant with early modern anxieties about the tongue's quasi-autonomy, this simile expresses the way in which, though Honorea's raucous behaviour makes her appear to be individualistically opposing the norms of her male milieu, in fact she is not in control of her tongue. By implication, Honorea's body becomes the static 'tree' that simply supports a clattering object. Chapman's character Ero, drawing on ideas purportedly deriving from Aristotle, states 'when a man dies, the last thing that moves is his heart; in a woman her tongue', comparing the woman's tongue to spiders' legs uncannily moving after death.[67] Anger appreciates the tongue's ability to rebel against the speaker, comparing the aggrieved woman, the loquacious man, and the 'slanderous tongue' to deadly string-like animals: the snake and the eel. Recognising the inefficacy of his previously-vaunted 'force', Belphagor complains,

> May he ne're speak that makes a Woman speak,
> She talks now, sure for all the time that's past,
> Her Tongue is like a Scare crow in a tree,
> That clatters still with every puff of winde;
> I have so haunted her from place to place,
> About the hall from thence into the parler,
> Up to the Chamber, down into the Garden,
> And still she railes and chafes and scoulds,
> As if it were the Sessions day in hell,
> Yet will I haunt her with an open mouth,
> And never leave her till I force her love me.[68]

As she scolds, Honorea embodies searing, surging vitality: 'chaf[ing]' once again and also 'rail[ing]' which at the time could mean gushing, ranting, and wandering to and fro.[69] Her vitality is simultaneously limited as an expression of her own power and agency, because her tongue is described as an instrument played by an external body. The demonic counterpart to Dunstan's harp that mysteriously plays by itself, Honorea's tongue 'clatters still with every puff of winde' rather than being guided by her own inner intentions. Like the harp, which was played by a devilish trick effected through stage-trickery, Honorea's shrewish vitality is an opportunity for both Belphagor and the actor playing Honorea to show how they can 'play' her. Unlike Dunstan's harp, and unlike Machiavelli's Belfagor who controls the people he possesses (getting them to discourse on philosophy, speak Latin, and reveal their sins) Honorea's tongue proves too much for Belphagor to control.[70] Simultaneously the actor playing Honorea has the opportunity to embody what Wojciehowski calls 'an onrush of vitality' and transmit it to the audience. Wojciehowski argues that audiences can feel an exhilarated release when characters move 'from a less vital state' of stillness and silence into 'a more vital state' of speech and movement.[71] She describes this as 'a mirrored sensation of intensifying aliveness', and emphasises that it is appreciated and experienced with 'immediacy' and without the need for conscious appraisal of the situation.[72] Honorea's outburst seems calculated less to teach audiences about ideal female behaviour than to provoke an immediate response to her 'intensifying aliveness'.

Belphagor over-optimistically aims to 'force her love me'; having boasted of his skill over the harp, he never attains his goal of taming Honorea's will. *Grim* leads us to appreciate the ways in which Honorea is different from the harp. The stop and start of the harp becomes a small appetiser to the main show: Honorea's seemingly uncontrollable clattering, chafing, and angry shouting. Belphagor's binding and loosing of Honorea is complicated and thwarted by Honorea's own desires and preferences, notably her lovesickness for Musgrave; at one point, 'the devil' (Belphagor?) disguises himself as Musgrave and coldly rejects a desperate Honorea, to try and break her heart. Ultimately, *Grim* locates supreme power not in Honorea's body but in God. Honorea attempted to claim control of her life in Act I: 'you may elect for me but I'll dispose'. In Act IV, congratulated by Lacy, Dunstan reframes this statement, 'God doth dispose all at his blessed will'.[73] This repetition of the word 'dispose' emphasises that the agent in control of Honorea's life story is God, not Honorea herself.

Vitality: Outside of Language

Stern writes that though we can attempt to describe vitality forms in language, doing so has a deadening effect on vitality. Stern states, 'the vitality forms are not readily describable in words or mathematics. Moreover, when they are so described, and they can be, they lose most of their ability to evoke'.[74] The characters in *Grim* attempt to narrate vitality, describing bodies tied, loosed, chafing, swooning, weak, sick, older, haltered, stitched, laying about, overcome by sleep. At several points, Honorea's forms of vitality belie the vocabulary used to describe her: when she seems loose she may be bound to the devil; when the male characters 'tye' her to Lacy her body visibly and disobediently grieves. Honorea's initial desire to marry Musgrave is clear from her 'weeping' when she is on the brink of marrying Lacy at the start of the play; later she confirms this by exclaiming that Musgrave is her 'love' and anxiously pursuing the devil disguised as Musgrave.[75] When (re-)tamed by Dunstan, Honorea's final bodily acts (fainting and weeping) are ambiguous.

Towards the end of the play, Honorea believes that Lacy has died and Marian urges her to rejoice in her freedom: 'Now Honorea we are freed from blame| And both enrich'd with happy widows name'.[76] Lacy promptly enters, alive and well, to inform them that he is 'revived again'; Honorea's immediate response is to cry and fall: 'Marian, I shed some tears of perfect grief [*She falleth into a Sound*]'.[77] Honorea makes her loss of vitality legible as sheer disappointment, distress, and dismay to hear that her unwanted suitor is still hovering round, bent on marrying her. Marian swiftly re-interprets Honorea's faint in a way more acceptable to Lacy, informing him that Honorea is 'half dead to hear of your untimely end'. Honorea swiftly accepts this cue, by addressing her continued ability to speak while emphasising her tongue's insufficiency and her dependency on Lacy: 'my tongue's not able to report| Those joys my heart conceives to see thee live'.[78] As Morgan and Lacy want, ultimately Honorea can speak just enough to affirm the 'bind[ing]' marriage contract with Lacy, but not so much that she disruptively asserts her own will. Honorea makes her faint legible to Lacy as a maritorious response; she relies on available cultural ideas of tongue-tied lovers sapped of their vitality to re-position her fall as being 'half dead' through love. In Philemon Holland's translation of Sappho 31 in *The Philosophie* (1603), the first into English, a lover lies breathless in 'exstasie' and 'fading' as if dead ('Withouten sense and breath I lie as if death of me sudennly| Surprize had made'); their 'dissolved' (not necessarily 'liquefied', but rather untied, weakened, relaxed, softened, or detached) tongue strings one of several symptoms of their love alongside fiery blushes, quaking flesh, shaking sinews, and buzzing ears:

> Thy face no sooner doe I see,
> But sudden silence comes on me;
> My tongue strings all dissolved bee,
> And speech quite gone . . .

Holland uses the sudden shortness of the final two-foot line of each stanza to perform the 'silence' and 'surprise' he typically describes in these lines.[79]

Though towards the end of the trajectory of her swoon Honorea positions herself as a tongue-tied lover like Sappho's, her first words when she swoons tell a contrary tale about her plummeting vitality: she is enervated at the despairing thought of marrying Lacy. As Francis Bacon states in a posthumously published speech to the House of Commons, 'in Consent, where *Tongue strings*, not *Hart-strings*, make the *Musick*; That *Harmony* may end in *Discord*'.[80] For Lyne, swooning can show us 'the boundary of vitality' as vitality 'ebbs' away when a character faints.[81] Lacy has to ask Honorea to 'look on me': perhaps she is still attempting to master her dismay and disgust and cannot turn her face to his.[82] Those of us who look on Honorea – in theatres or in our minds' eye – are offered opportunities for complex kinesic responses. Here is a woman who purports to be tamed but who is sapped of her strength and will as she faces her unwanted marital future, who surged forth with the devil's drink, then later was offered a short-lived prospect of joyful release at Lacy's supposed death. Here – despite many early modern texts including this play linking heart-strings, tongue-strings, and musical strings – is a broken-hearted human, not a harp.[83]

Conclusion

Communicating an onrush of vitality to the audience, Honorea seems ostensibly to be gloriously breaking patriarchal codes of behaviour when she bursts into angry speech. However, the play complicates this as she suffers potential possession by a devil, and (re)possession by God and by Lacy as her husband. Even Honorea's vitality is not completely her own: we might attribute it to Belphagor's power over her. Keeping our eyes on Honorea's vitality has revealed the impact that Dunstan, Morgan, and Lacy's patriarchal narratives have on her as an individual. Tracking the weakening of Honorea's vitality when she faints at Lacy's revival reveals her broken heart. This moment, no matter what gloss she and Marian later put on it, can speak kinesically, and poignantly, to both modern and early modern audiences. No matter how much Honorea may glibly insist that she faints for joy at the prospect of marrying Lacy, her body's cues speak more loudly, nudging us to draw on our own kinaesthetic and kinesis understanding to read her faint as one of despair.

As my analysis of bodily behaviours in previous chapters did, my parsing of Honorea's vitality has rested on kinesic and kinaesthetic understanding in conjunction with readings of literary and theological texts. Texts ranging from the Bible to Machiavelli's *Belfagor* have illuminated the complex – and blurry – divine and diabolic contest at play in the binding and loosening of Honorea. Filtered through literary texts, Honorea's vitality is shaped and embellished by the very language it challenges. Spenser's Malbecco is responsible for Belphagor's intrusion into Honorea's world. Turning to the episode in which Malbecco appears in *The Faerie Queene* suggests parallels between Spenser's representation of the elderly avaricious Malbecco and young free-spirited Hellenore 'unfitly yokt together in one teeme', and I. T.'s depiction of Honorea yoked to her older husband Lacy.[84] Malbecco's fate as he is cuckolded (nine times in one particular night) by Hellenore results in the question posed at the start of *Grim*: did Malbecco kill himself, or did Hellenore kill him? That is, are free-spirited and sexually 'loose' women so terrible that they override men's decision-making power and drive men to despair? At the end of *Grim*, Honorea too implicitly poses a question. We have seen her tongue and behaviour bound (both by nature and by Dunstan channelling divine power), and loose, on the rampage. When Honorea is re-bound by Dunstan, flickers of her autonomy seem to remain, and I wonder if in a sequel they would kindle into fury once more. Despite Dunstan's best efforts, will Honorea and Lacy end up like Hellenore and Malbecco: she following her own devilish will, and he a desperate cuckold? *Grim* leaves the matter somewhat open.

Notes

1. I. T., 'Grim the Collier of Croyden; or, The Devil and His Dame: With the Devil and St Dunstan', in *Gratiae Theatrales* (London: RD, 1662) (G1r-K3r), G8v-G9r.
2. OED, 'chafe' *n*1. This sense of 'chafe' was current throughout the mid-16th to mid-19th centuries, first recorded in 1551. www.oed.com [accessed 02.03.2020].
3. OED, 'chafe', *v*1–2, 5, 6a, 7, 10. www.oed.com [accessed 02.03.2020].
4. Edmund Spenser, *The Faerie Queene* (London: Richard Field, 1596). I refer to the 1596 edition as it contains all books (I-VI). The earlier 1590 version included only books I-III.
5. He wants to 'live in sweet contentment with my wife,| That when I back again return to hell| All women may be bound to reverence me| For saving of their credits as I will', I. T., 'Grim the Collier; G6r.
6. I. T., 'Grim the Collier', I7v.
7. *Holy Bible*, Geneva Version, 1599. All subsequent references in this chapter are to the 1599 Geneva bible.
8. Cited in Kate Aughterson, ed., *Renaissance Woman: A Sourcebook: Constructions of Femininity in England* (London: Routledge, 1995), 32.
9. I. T., 'Grim the Collier', G5v.
10. Robert Shuler, 'Bewitching the Shrew', *Texas Studies in Literature and Language* 46(4) (2004), 387–431. Melissa Hull Geil discusses the trope in early jest books, and discusses the ways in which early modern women's silence could signify obedience and resistance ('Mutism and Feminine Silence: Gender, Performance, and Disability in *Epicoene*', in *Performing Disability*, 98–121).
11. Ben Jonson, 'The Devil Is an Ass', in *The Works of Benjamin Jonson* (London: John Beale et al., 1641), Q1r. There are further similarities between Jonson's play and *Grim*; for instance, like Belphagor Pug suffers human weaknesses and emotions on taking human form, and Jonson's character Fitzdotterel forces his wife to stand silent as he and Wittipol speak for and about her.
12. '[T]he deuyls complayne| That women put them to suche payne| By theyr condicions so croked and crabbed| Frowardly fashonde so waywarde and wrabbed| So farre in deuision and sturrynge suche stryfe| That all the deuyls be wery of theyr lyfe', John Heywood, *The Playe Called the Foure PP* (London: William Middleton, 1544), D4v. Points of connection between *Grim* and contemporary shrew-taming plays suggest a set of images common to shrew and devil plays. For instance, John Fletcher's

character Petronius refers curiously to St Dunstan tweaking the devil's nose in *The Tamer Tamed* (1611); Dunstan's slapstick rumbles with the devil are central to *Grim the Collier*. 'That blessing that St Dunstan gave the devil,| If I were near thee, I would give thee -| Pull thee down by th' nose', John Fletcher, *The Woman's Prize or The Tamer Tamed* (London: for Humphrey Robinson and Humphrey Mosley, 1647), Nnnnn3r.
13. Thus, in John Lacey's 1667 adaptation of Shakespeare's *The Taming of the Shrew*, Petruchio's wife is a 'devil' but also 'the Devil's Dam', while Petruchio is both the devil's 'bridegroome' and a 'devil' himself, John Lacey, *Sauny the Scott* (London: E Whitlock, 1698), D1v.
14. Machiavelli 'Belphagor', in J. R. Hale trans. and ed., *The Literary Works of Machiavelli* (Oxford: Oxford University Press, 1961) (191–202), 193. Machiavelli's novel was translated into English as *The Devil a Married Man* (1647) and adapted twice more for the seventeenth-century stage (the anonymous closet drama *The Devil and the Parliament*, 1648; J Wilson's *Belfagor*, 1691). D. W. Thompson traces the tale's folkloric provenance in 'Belphagor in *Grim the Collier* and *Riche's Farewell*', MLN 50(2) (1935), 99–102.
15. I. T., 'Grim the Collier', G4r.
16. For Sante Matteo, this reflects Machiavelli's wider interest in the meaninglessness of language, 'To Hell with Men and Meaning! Vesting Authority in Machiavelli's *Belfagor*', *Italica* 79(1) (2002) (1–22), 7.
17. Barnabe Riche, *Riche his Farewel to Militarie Profesion* (London: J Kingston, 1583), Dd2v. Thompson discusses Riche's stronger influence from Straparola rather than Machiavelli.
18. For discussion, see 'Devil and his Dame', in Roslyn Knutson, David McInnis, and Matthew Steggle, eds, Lost Plays Database, https://lostplays.folger.edu/Devil_and_his_Dame [accessed 03.03.2020]; David Kathman, 'Haughton, William' (2013), *Oxford Dictionary of National Biography*, https://doi.org/10.1093/ref:odnb/12617 [accessed 03.03.2020]. On a potential later version see Frederick Burwick, *Drama of the Industrial Revolution* (Cambridge: Cambridge University Press, 2015), 137–8. In a short section on *Grim the Collier*, E. K. Chambers notes that some critical discussion related *Grim*'s first performance to speculations about the revival of *Like Will to Like* at the Rose by Pembroke's Men in 1600 (*The Elizabethan Stage* [Oxford: Clarendon, 1923], vol. 4, 16).
19. H. Dugdale Sykes, 'The Authorship of "Grim, the Collier of Croydon"', *The MLR* 14(3) (1919), 245–53; William Baillie, 'The Date and Authorship of *Grim the Collier of Croydon*', *Modern Philology* 76(2) (1978), 179–84, 180. Bailie's statement that *Grim* was a key source for *Wily Beguiled* (1606) seems unconvincing, substantiated only by Robin Goodfellow's appearance in both plays. In 1691, Gerard Langbaine conflates *Grim*'s 'I. T.' with a J. T associated with a 1686 translation of Seneca's *Troas*, Gerard Langbaine, *An Account of the English Dramatick Poets* (Oxford: L. L., 1691), Kk6r. Langbaine seems mistaken here: the translator 'J. Ta' appearing on this *Troas*'s frontispiece is sometimes identified as a James Talbot (d. 1708) who also translated Horace. Another 'J. T.' linked to *Troas* is Jacob Tonson the elder (1655/6–1736), a bookseller specialising in translations of the classics, for whom *Troas* was originally printed.

20. William King briefly mentions *Grim the Collier* in *Dialogues of the Dead* (London: A Baldwin, 1699), L4v; the relevant dialogue, between Dekker and Flecknoe's ghosts, dates *Grim* after *Gammer Gurton's Needle* (1575). *Grim the Collier* was revived onstage in 1774; Robert Dodlsey's 1744 edition was revived by William Hazlitt in 1874, followed by John Farmer's 1908 *Five Anonymous Plays* (1908), and Baillie's 1984 edition of *Gratiae Theatrales*. Late nineteenth and early twentieth-century letter writers' murmurs about *Grim the Collier* in *Notes and Queries* mainly ask if anyone has heard of this lesser known play, or the plant of the same name. For example, M. P. asks 'Does any reader of "N&Q" know a little book on this subject', calling *Grim the Collier* 'a humorous comedy popular in Queen Elizabeth's reign' (August 14th 1880, *Notes and Queries* vol. 56-II, 128). Evan Thomas replies referring M. P. to Hazlitt's edition of Dodley's *Collection of Old English Plays* (September 18th 1880, *Notes and Queries* vol. 56-II, Issue 38, 234).
21. For discussion of Grim see Laura Seymour 'The Name of Grim: Tracing the Character of Grim the Collier in Sixteenth- and Seventeenth-Century English Plays', *Early Theater* 24(2) (2021), 55–71.
22. I. T., 'Grim the Collier', G11r, I5v.
23. Ronald Rittgers, *The Reformation of the Keys: Confession, Conscience, and Authority in Sixteenth-Century Germany* (Harvard University Press, 2004), 98.
24. Rittgers, *The Reformation of the Keys*, 3, 79, 99.
25. Woods, *Shakespeare's Unreformed Fictions*, 1, 16–17. See e.g., Woods's chapter 'Affecting Possession in *King Lear*', *Shakespeare's Unreformed Fictions*, 133–168.
26. Richard Hiers, '"Binding" and "Loosing": The Matthean Authorisations', *Journal of Biblical Literature* 104(2) (1985) (233–50), 239.
27. Hiers, 'Binding and Loosing', 238.
28. For Croesus' son, 'his tongue-strings unloosed', see e.g., *Thomas Brooks, The Crown and Glory of Christianity* (London: H Crips, J Sims and H Mortlock, 1662), T3r. In George Wilkins' translation of Justinian, Battas' 'tongue stringes loosed ... encouraged [his companions'] harts', serving as inspiration for others, *The History of Justine* (London: William Jaggard, 1606), L6v. Cf. Steven Connor, Beyond Words (London: Reaktion, 2014), 17–32.
29. I. T., 'Grim the Collier', G7v.
30. I. T., 'Grim the Collier', G5r.
31. I. T., 'Grim the Collier', K1r.
32. I. T., 'Grim the Collier', G2v.
33. I. T., 'Grim the Collier', G4r.
34. Daniel Stern, *Forms of Vitality: Exploring Dynamic Experience in Psychology, the Arts, Psychotherapy, and Development* (Oxford: Oxford University Press, 2010), 149, 7. For descriptions of vitality: Cf e.g., Gärd Holmqvist et al., 'Expressions of Vitality Affects and Basic Affects During Art Therapy and Their Meaning for Inner Change', *International Journal of Art Therapy* 24(1) (2009) (30–39), 31–2.
35. Stern, *Forms of Vitality*, 98.
36. Stern, *Forms of Vitality*, 75–6, 98.

37. Hannah Chapelle Wojciehowski, 'Statues that Move: Vitality Effects in *The Winter's Tale*', *Literature and Theology* 28(3) (299–315), 301–2. She adds (302) that performers can find physical and emotional pleasure in holding the pose of a living statue.
38. Raphael Lyne, 'Shakespeare's Vital Signs', in Timothy Chesters and Kathryn Banks, eds, *Movement in Renaissance Literature: Exploring Kinesic Intelligence* (New York: Palgrave Macmillan, 2017), 189–212.
39. E. g., Wojciehowski, 'Statues that Move', 303.
40. Stern, *Forms of Vitality*, 7. I have modified the format of this list slightly in that Stern originally presents it as bullet points.
41. Stern, *Forms of Vitality*, 8.
42. I. T., 'Grim the Collier', H10r.
43. I. T., 'Grim the Collier', I5r.
44. I. T., 'Grim the Collier', I5v.
45. See Carla Mazzio, 'Sins of the Tongue in Early Modern England', *Modern Language Studies* 28(3/4) (1998) (93–124), 98.
46. I am very grateful to Jack Christie for this suggestion in our MA class on *Grim*.
47. I. T., 'Grim the Collier', G8v.
48. I. T., 'Grim the Collier', G8v.
49. I. T., 'Grim the Collier', G8v.
50. I. T., 'Grim the Collier', G7r.
51. Morgan describes Honorea's non-verbal state as an 'infelicit[y]' (contrasting it with her etymologically-cognate 'happiness' in marrying Lacy), needing 'recovery', even as he and Lacy glory in, and take advantage of, the fact she does not speak. I. T., 'Grim the Collier', G4v.
52. I. T., 'Grim the Collier', G5r. Later editor John Farmer amends 'impose on' to 'imprison', Anon, 'Grim the Collier of Croydon', in John Farmer, ed., *Five Anonymous Plays* (Guildford: Charles W. Traylen, 1966 [facsimile of the English Drama Society's 1908 edition]), 110.
53. I. T., 'Grim the Collier', G9r. Dunstan specifically enters with his beads so they are key to his costume (I. T., 'Grim the Collier', G2r).
54. Spenser, *Faerie Queene*, II.iv.12–15. I am very grateful to Joe Moshenska for the suggestion to look at this reference.
55. Spenser, *Faerie Queene*, II.iv.11.
56. Jane Anger, *Her Protection for Women* (London: Richard Jones and Thomas Orwin, 1589), A4v. Anne Lake Prescott argues that though nothing is known of Jane Anger beyond this pamphlet, the author is probably providing their real name (Anger being a common surname in early modern England) and making use of the potential it provided to pun on her 'angry' state of mind ('it was ANGER that did write') and the anger she will provoke, 'ANGER shal reape anger for not agreeing with diseased persons' (Anger, *Her Protection for Women*, A4r; Anne Lake Prescott, 'Anger, Jane, fl. 1588', *Oxford Dictionary of National Biography* [2004] https://doi.org/10.1093/ref:odnb/39675 [accessed 02.02.2020]). It's possible that this text was published as part of a pair of texts by different authors in debate with each other, the stridency of the discourse amplified to attract readers, and their money.
57. Anger, *Her Protection for Women*, B1r.

58. Anger, *Her Protection for Women*, A4v.
59. Anger, *Her Protection for Women*, B4r-v.
60. Chapman's widows Eudora and Cynthia renege on their vows never to remarry. Cynthia reneges when her maid Ero's tongue is loosened by drink. Ero hints that she needs wine to oil her tongue 'O, I have lost my tongue in this same limbo;| The spring on't's spoiled, methinks it goes not off| With the old twang', adding 'I feare me thy lips haue gone so oft to the bottle, that thy tongue-strings are come broken home, and later describing it (in an image reminiscent, as we shall see of Honorea's tongue, clattering like a foreign object in her skull) as a suspicious object contained within her mouth rather than an integrated part of her body, 'Faith the truth is, my tongue hath beene so long tied vp, that tis couer'd with rust, & I rub it against my pallat as wee doe suspected coines, to trie whether it bee currant or no'; Lysander offers her drink to 'oil' her tongue and 'make it slide well', George Chapman, *The Widowes Teares a comedie* (London: William Stansby, 1612), H3v, H4v. A good grieving widow might allow her heartstrings to break, but a drunken, lax woman lets her tongue strings break, indicating both slurred and morally suspect speech. William L'Isle's translation of Du Bartas describes the drunken Noah (and drunkards in general) thus, 'His tongue-strings ouerwet doe cause him lisp and stut;| No word flies through his teeth, but witlesse, broke and cut', *Part of Du Bartas English and French* (London; Sarah Griffin, 1657), H1r. At the end of *The Widow's Teares*, 'Eudora whispers to Cynthia', suggesting the widows' confederacy and lack of interest in, or attention to, the men's sententious pronouncements against their undesirable behaviour. We cannot 'hear' the content of the whisper: the playtext does not detail what the women say. Mysterious, subversive, out of reach by the neat male attempt to control the play's conclusion, this whisper shows the undimmed power of female speech. Chapman, *The Widowes Teares*, L2v.
61. Anger, *Her Protection for Women*, B1r.
62. I. T., 'Grim the Collier', G9r.
63. I. T. 'Grim the Collier', H10r. Farmer moves the stage direction to after 'I'll stop your speech'; 'Grim the Collier', 146.
64. I. T., 'Grim the Collier', H10r.
65. I. T., 'Grim the Collier', G12v.
66. George Withers' early seventeenth-century 'emblem of the Evil tongue', a winged, disembodied tongue soaring across the land with 'unruly motion', exemplifies these anxieties; see Mazzio, 'Sins of the Tongue', 94–5, 100–1.
67. Chapman, *The Widowes Teares*, H3v; Akihiro Yamada affirms that though proverbially taken as Aristotle's this idea does not obviously stem from Aristotle, see note on George Chapman, *The Widow's Tears*, ed. Akihiro Yamada (Manchester: Manchester University Press, 1975), 4.2.155–6.
68. I. T., 'Grim the Collier', G11v.
69. OED, 'rail', *v.* 3–5, oed.com [accessed 04.03.2020].
70. Machiavelli, 'Belfagor', 199. For Matteo, Belfagor's control of his victims' speech reflects Machiavelli's wider interest in the meaninglessness of language, 'To Hell with Men and Meaning!', 15–16.
71. Wojciehowski, 'Statues that Move', 302.
72. Wojciehowski, 'Statues that Move', 308.

73. Anon, 'Grim the Collier', G6r.
74. Stern, *Forms of Vitality*, 97.
75. Farmer cuts the stage direction 'weeping' but preserves Clinton's 'your lady weeps, and know not what to do'; Anon, 'Grim the Collier', 113, 131, 141–2.
76. I. T., 'Grim the Collier', K1r.
77. I. T., 'Grim the Collier', K1r.
78. I. T., 'Grim the Collier', K1r.
79. Philemon Holland, *The philosophie, commonlie called, the morals vvritten by the learned philosopher Plutarch of Chaeronea* (London: Arnold Hatfield, 1603), Ddddd4v. See OED, 'dissolve', *v*., oed.com [accessed 04.03.2020]. Holland developed this translation through engaging with Jacques Amyot's 1572 French version. Thank you to Tania Demetriou for elucidating this translation and Emily Formstone for discussing it with me. Cf Tania Demetriou and Rowan Tomlinson, 'Introduction', in Tania Demetriou and Rowan Tomlinson, eds, *The Culture of Translation in Early Modern England and France 1500–1660* (Basingstoke: Palgrave Macmillan, 2015) (pp. 1–21), 3.
80. Bacon links the bonds between king and subject to those between families and households, stating that with King and Subject 'the Bonds are more special, but not so Forcible'. Francis Bacon, 'A *Speech*, of the *Kings Sollicitor*, perswading the *House* of *Commons*, to desist from further Question, of receiving the *Kings Messages*, by their *Speaker*', in William Rawley, *Resusitatio* (London: Sarah Griffin, 1657), G3r-G4r.
81. Lyne, 'Shakespearean Vital Signs', 199.
82. I. T., 'Grim the Collier', K1r.
83. In one translation of Psalm 51, the line usually translated 'open my lips' becomes 'thou wilt be pleased to open my lips, and to vntie my tongue strings', IB (attributed variously to John Bate and John Bennet). *The Psalme of Mercy, or a Meditation on Psalme 51* (London: Felix Kynaston, 1625) Q11r. In his alphabetical list of bons mots, under 'Thanksgiving', Robert Port writes, 'In thanksgiving heart-strings and tongue-strings should be tun'd to our soules' (*Spiritual Flowers for Saints and Sinners* [London: G. Dawson, 1655], G1r). In a 1661 hellfire sermon celebrating the Restoration, tongue and heart strings ideally make harp-like melodies now the people are physically untied from their 'Fetters': 'have we neither heart-strings, nor tongue-strings to make melody upon such occasions?' (Thomas Reeve, *England's beauty in seeing King Charles the Second restored to majesty preached by Tho. Reeve . . . in the parish church of Waltham Abbey in the county of Essex* [London: Sarah Griffin, 1657], C3r). In *The Widow's Tears*, Chapman refers to the wounds of a murder victim being 'tongu-tied', unable to reveal the murderer (5.5.111), recalling Shakespeare's description of Julius Caesar's wounds as 'dumb mouths', enlivened by others' tongues (3.2.217–21).
84. Spenser, *The Faerie Queene*, III.ix.6.

Index

'A Paper shewing how the Servants of the Lord was beaten as they are now', 67–8
Adams, Thomas, 84
Admiral's men, 85
Akercock (character), 83–5
Alemán, Mateo, *Guzmán de Alfarache*, 36–57
Ameka, Felix, 22, 34n
Anger, Jane, 99
 Her Protection for Women, 95–7, 106n
'Arancel de Necedades', 50
Ardolino, Frank, 14
Aristotle, 60–2, 78n, 99, 107n
 Rhetoric, 39
Aristotle's Master-Piece, 78n
Askew, Egeon, *Brotherly Reconcilement*, 45
asyndetic clauses, 44
authentic shaping, 74–6

Bacon, Francis, 101, 108n
Baker, Naomi, 69–70
beggars' book, 43–50
Belphagor (character), 82–108, 103n
Bible, 83, 87–8, 102, 108n
 and walking, 44–5
Blankaart, Stephen, 78n
Bolens, Guillemette, 3–4, 7n, 9–10, 25
 The Style of Gestures, 4
bound body, 81–108
Braithwaite, Richard, 'Of Sleepe', 21
Brome, Richard, *The Late Lancashire Witches*, 28–9

Bruder Rausch (character), 13–15, 32n
Bugg, Francis
 The Character of a Quaker, 62–3
 A Retrospective Glass for the Quakers, 67

Calvinism, 86
Castiliano (character), 81–108
Catholicism, 14, 21–2, 31n, 37, 41, 86–7
Cave, Terence, *Thinking with Literature*, 3–4
chafing, 82
Chapman, George, *The Widow's Tears*, 96, 98–9, 107n, 108n
chastity, 81–108
children
 naughty, 43–4, 47
 walking, 43–6
Cho, Nancy Jiwon, 66
Christmas games, 13
church strut, 36–9, 41–2, 47, 51–3
class, 61–3, 65, 67, 69–70, 73, 74, 79n
cognitive literary theorists, 3–4
Coker, Lauren, 47
comic exaggeration, 3
constancy, 75
conversos, 41
 queer, 53
creative writing, 66

Dekker, Thomas, *If This Be Not a Good Play, the Devil Is in It*, 8–35
Dekker his Dreame, 26–7
demonic possession, 2, 33n, 86–8

demons, 12, 14, 93
  exorcism, 86–7
  and women, 33n, 88, 99
devil, and women, 81–108
devil plays, 13–14
devil saying grace, 12–20
Digges, Leonard, 41, 55n
disability, 47–50
docility, 81–108
double-prefixing, 10
Du Bartas, 107n
Dunstan (character), 83, 86–96, 99–100, 102–3, 104n

eating animals, 11, 32n
Ellwood, Thomas, 6n
  The History of the Life of Thomas Ellwood, 1–2, 58–80
Ellwood, Walter, 1–2, 58–80, 77n
Erasmus, Desiderius, *The Godly Feast*, 31n
Eucharist, 8–29
exorcism, 87

fake pliancy, 74–6
false Quakers, 74–6
Fletcher, John, *The Woman's Prize or The Tamer Tamed*, 104n
flexibility, 63–4
Fonesca, Cristóbal de, *Discursos*, 40–1
Fox, George, 60, 67

gait, 36–57
Gammer Gurton's Needle, 13–14, 22
Geil, Melissa Hull, 103n
Giles, Ryan, 42
Glanvill, Joseph, 62
  The Vanity of Dogmatizing, 78n
grace, 8–35
  devil saying, 12–20
Gratiae Theatrales, 85, 97
Gregory the Great, 33n
Griffith, Eva, 13, 25–6

habits, 3, 60–2, 78n
  non-conformist, 58–80
hat honour, 67, 77n
Haughton, William, 85
Haydock, Richard, 65

Healey, Robynne Rogers, 80n
Henslowe, Philip, 85
Heywood, John, *The Playe Called the Foure PP*, 84, 103–4n
Heywood, Thomas
  The Late Lancashire Witches, 28–9
  A Pleasant Conceited Comedy, Wherein Is Shewed How a Man May Chuse a Good Wife From a Bad, 18–19, 25
Hiers, Richard, 86–7
Holland, Philemon, *The Philosophie*, 101
Honorea (character), 81–108
humanism, 31n
hunger, 8–24

I. T., *Grim the Collier of Croydon; or, The Devil and His Dame*, 13–14, 81–108

Jeannerod, Mark, 78n
jest books, 103n
Jews, 37, 43
Jonson, Ben, *The Devil Is an Ass*, 13–14, 84, 103n

Kendall, Timothy
  Flowers of Epigrammes, 32n
  'Of saying grace,' 11
kinaesthetic experience, 51
kinaesthetic imagination, 8
kinaesthetic intelligence, 25
kinaesthetic knowledge, 4
kinaesthetic learning, 36–58
kinaesthetic melodies, 3, 4, 59–60
kinaesthetic understanding, 102
kinesic experience, 51
kinesic intelligence, 4, 25
kinesic learning, 36–58
kinesic melodies, 59–60
kinesic responses, 101
kinesic understanding, 102
'kinetic melody', 7n
Koptjevskaja-Tamm, Maria, 22
  The Linguistics of Temperature, 34n

Lacey, John, 104n
Langbaine, Gerard, 104n

Index

Liapi, Lena, 40
L'Isle, William, 107n
lists, 95–6
Lomazzo, G. P., *A Tracted Containing the Arts of Curious Painting, Carving and Building*, 65
loosed body, 81–108
Lutheranism, 86
Lyne, Raphael, 90, 101

Mabbe, James
   Deuout Contemplations, 40–1
   The Rogue, 36–57
Machiavelli, Niccolò, *Belfagor Arcidiavolo*, 85, 102, 104n, 107n
Malabou, Catherine, 61–2, 64–6, 74–6, 78n
   The Future of Hegel, 61–2
Malbecco (character), 82–3, 94, 102
Marlowe, Christopher, *Dr Faustus*, 13, 17–18
masculinity, 60, 69–74
   rhyming, 63
Matos, Carlos Antonio Rodríguez, 53
McConachie, Bruce, 74
metaphoricity, 39
Milton, John, 59
   Paradise Regained, 66
mimicry, 38, 53–4
miracle-cure, 47–9, 87–8
mistrusting the self, 27–9
monks, 8–35, 31n
Moore, Richard, 79n
Munro, Lucy, 10
Musgrave (character), 81, 100

naughty children, 43–4, 47
non-conformist, habits, 58–80

Orwin, Thomas, 'His Surfeit in Love', 96
Ovid, 26

'peace and quietness', 65–9
Penington, Giuli, 59, 73–4
Penington, Isaac, 59, 70, 79n
Penington, Mary, 59, 66, 69–70
Penington, Mary (junior), 63, 79–80n
physical combat, 70–4

plain plasticity, 58–80
plastic power, 62, 65–6, 78n
polyptoton, 2
Port, Robert, 108n
Porter, Endymion, 26–7
prefixes, 13
   double, 10
Prescott, Anne Lake, 106n
Priebsch, Robert, 15
'proface', 9
proprioception, 8–35
proprioceptive language, 8, 25
prosthetics, 8
Protestantism, 8, 14, 25, 31n, 86–7
pyrotechnics, 8, 12

Quakers, 1–2, 6n, 58–80
queer converso, 53

R. H., *The Character of a Quaker*, 60
Rabelais, François, *Gargantua and Pantagruel*, 31n
Rance, John, 58–9
'reading' bodies, 4
Red Bull Theatre, London, 8, 12–13, 26, 30–1n
Reeve, Thomas, 108n
Reformation, 86–7
Reillo, Giorgio, 41
rhyming, 10–11, 30
   masculinity, 63
Riche, Barnabe, *Riche's Farewell to The Military Profession*, 85
Rittgers, Ronald, 86
Rokotnitz, Naomi, 4, 7n
Roodenberg, Herman, 77n
Row-Heyveld, Lindsey, 47–8
Rush, Friar (character), 8–35, 32n

Schaap Williams, Katherine, 47–8
Scot, Reginald, *Discoverie of Witchcraft*, 13
selfhood, 64–5
self-shaping, 69–74
self-touching, 10
sensorimotor responses, 4–5, 74
Shacklesoul (character), 12–20, 23, 30
Shakespeare, William
   Henry IV, 31n

Shakespeare, William (*cont.*)
  The Taming of the Shrew, 98, 104n
  The Winter's Tale, 90
Sheets-Johnstone, Maxine, 90
  L'humour et le savoir des corps, 4
  The Primacy of Movement, 3
shrewishness, 83–6, 93, 98–9, 103–4n
Shuler, Robert, 84
silence, 81–108
Smith, Nigel, 67
Spanish Inquisition, 37
'Spanishness,' 41
Spenser, Edmund, *The Faerie Queene*, 82–3, 94–5, 102
Spolsky, Ellen, 9–10, 39–40, 49
St Augustine, 25
Stern, Daniel, 90–1, 100
Straparola, Giovanni Frecesco, *Le Piacevoli Notti*, 85
Straznicky, Marta, 30–1n
'swerve', 49

Targoff, Ramie, 60
taste, 8–11, 8–35
Tatham, John, 85
temperature, 8–11, 20–7, 29–30, 33n, 34n
temptation, 17–18, 29, 30
The Historie of Frier Rush, 15
The Historie of the damnable life and deserved death of Doctor John Faustus, 18, 33n
Throckmorton, Elizabeth, 17, 19
Tonson, Jacob, 104n
trust, 4, 7n

Vila, Juan Diego, 53
violence, 67–9, 70–4
Virgil, *Aeneid*, 45
Visser, Margaret, 19
vitality, 81–108

walking, 3, 36–57
witchcraft, 17, 28–9
Wojciehowski, Hannah Chapelle, 90, 98–9
women
  and demons, 33n, 88, 99
  and the devil, 81–108
Woods, Gillian, 25, 86
Wyeth, Joseph, 66–7

Yamada, Akihiro, 107n

EU representative:
Easy Access System Europe
Mustamäe tee 50, 10621 Tallinn, Estonia
Gpsr.requests@easproject.com

www.ingramcontent.com/pod-product-compliance
Lightning Source LLC
Chambersburg PA
CBHW070400240426
43671CB00013BA/2575